In the Event of a Water Landing

Michael G. Walling

To Steve,

Mentor and friend.

Thanks for being there for me.

Sincerely,

Mike

Walling, Michael G.

In the Event of a Water Landing

ISBN-10: 0982855303

ISBN-13: 978-098285530 0

Library Congress Control Number 2010910210

Cover design by Sunny Su (sunnysu@graphicartists.com)

Web site design by Lisa Adams (www.lisaadams.com)

Printed in the United States of America by Cutter Publishing (www.cutterpublishing.com) 2010

Visit www.cutterpublishing.com to order additional copies.

☙❧

Dedicated to

Chuck Martin and Mike Hall

Table of Contents

Acknowledgements

This book would not exist without the contributions and support of many people.

I am grateful first to my wife, Mary, whose unwavering encouragement insured that this project would be completed. She also provided the title for the book, one that never occurred to me.

For the *Bermuda Sky Queen* saga, I am indebted to Mike Hall, Chuck Martin, Keith Woodmansee, Bernard Brown, James Macdonald, the Ritchie family, and the late Phil Taylor for their remarkable memories of a truly remarkable event in which they all were heroic participants.

Thanks to Doak Walker, RM1, USCG (Retired) for his friendship and for introducing me to the USCGC *Pontchartrain* and *Sovereign of the Skies* crews and passengers. Among those from *Sovereign of the Skies* are Patricia Reynolds, Len Specia, Frank Garcia. Jr, Richard L. Brown, and the Gordons. From *Pontchartrain* there's Richard Olson in addition to Doak.

A very special thanks to Jay Spenser, Joe Sutter, Mary Kane, and Linda Lee of Boeing Commercial Airplanes. Their support and expertise was invaluable. No matter how busy their schedules, they took the time to help me out.

One of the greatest pleasures I had was in getting to know folks from Transocean Air Lines, Flying Tigers, TWA, and Pan Am. These include Arue Szura and Charles Mac Quarrie from Transocean; Flying Tigers Captain George Gewehr and Carol Gould Hansen; TWA's Robert Sherman and Robert Allardyce; and Captains Buck Clippard,

Stu Archer and Ed Dover from Pan Am among others. Also, Captain Elgen Long added his expertise with the Navigation chapter.

Contributions of time, material, and knowledge from Tara King, editor of the US Coast Guard Alumni Magazine; Bruce Kitt, Northwest Airlines Museum; Michael O'Leary, Editor, Challenge Publications; Jim Burin, Flight Safety Foundation; Jon Ostrower, Flight Global; Wendy Stafford, Flight Attendant Express; Cris Piquinela, Director of Business Development, Curtis Publishing, Jenifer Stepp at Stars and Stripes; and John from Century of Flight helped immensely in my research.

For the Aeroflot ditching in the Neva River, I am indebted to Konstantin F. Kulikov, District Manager, Aeroflot—Russian Airlines, General Representation in USA, New York, and Anatoly Ivanenko, Moscow Aeroflot Headquarters.

Every writer needs an editor. Sherri Hubble performed this task with great skill and tact.

As always, thanks to Sunny Su for her great cover design and to Lisa Adams for keeping the web sites up to date and looking fresh.

Preface

This book began over five years ago as a promise to Mike Hall to tell the story of the *Bermuda Sky Queen* ditching. I first heard about it from Mike while I was writing *Bloodstained Sea*. What was to be a simple narrative excursion became one of the most remarkably far ranging voyages of my life.

My research led to Bernard Brown, James Macdonald, and Phil Taylor from the Bibb. Keith Woodmansee was the first Sky Queen crew member I was able to locate. He, in turn, led me to Chuck Martin.

More fun came in conversations with Gordon Ritchie and his sister Heather. It was Heather who shared with me her mother's story about the ditching.

Next came Doak Walker and the Ponchartrain and Sovereign of the Skies crews and passengers, including the Gordons.

Now I had the core stories, but I needed information about aviation history, aircraft design, air navigation, and other people involved in ditchings. This is where the voyage really took off as I truly entered the world of flight. With each new contact I expanded my promise to write what had now become not only the *Bermuda Sky Queen* story, but also that of the *Sovereign of the Skies*, other remarkable ditching stories, and tales of many unknown or unrecognized chapters and people in aviation history.

All the stories make this work very personal to me. At times, particularly at the passing of Phil Taylor, it's been hard emotionally, but the price is always worth it. I try to write from my heart when telling the horrific tales of aircraft going down and people struggling to survive. To do anything less would betray the folks who told me what they went through and would cheat you as the reader.

This promise has taken me far longer to keep than I'd planned, but now the finished work is in your hands.

Mike Walling
Hudson, Massachusetts
June 2010

1. Introduction

Ditching:

A planned event in which a flight crew knowingly makes a controlled emergency landing in water.

National Transportation Safety Board of the United States (NTSB)

Flying, for many of us, is routine and not much fun. It's just a way of getting from one place to another quickly (sometimes) and it often entails a degree of discomfort in the process.

Until US Airways Flight 1549 went down in the Hudson River on January 16, 2009, many people thought the: "In event of water landing..." safety instructions were out-dated and just part of the speech left over from a distant time. According to the National Transportation Accident Report, 145 passenger interviews revealed that about 70 percent of the passengers did not watch any of the preflight safety demonstration. In addition, more than 90 percent did not read the safety information card before or during the flight. The NTSB believes that these responses clearly indicate that passenger safety information is still routinely ignored by most travelers.

Fortunately this most recent ditching was a complete success in that no lives were lost. This has not always been the case.

From 1934 until 2009 there have been 25 multi-engine commercial passenger aircraft ditchings for which I have found records. These ditchings did not include aircraft that wound up in shallow water at the end of a runway either through a missed approach or an overshot runway approach. Remarkably, 21 of the pilots put their aircraft down safely. It wasn't until after the plane was in the water that casualties occurred in 13 of these successful landings.

In the eight ditchings where no lives were lost, two have been in rivers, four in bays, and two in the open ocean. Seven of the eight were in calm water. The eighth is a whole different story. All eight successful ditchings have one thing in common—boats or ships nearby to effect the rescue.

The first of the eight completely successful ditchings occurred on April 25, 1938, roughly 10 miles southeast of Kingston, Jamaica. A Pan American Airways Sikorsky twin engine flying boat ditched in rough seas after losing power to one engine. The 12 passengers and four crew members where quickly rescued by a lifeboat from the nearby cargo ship Cavina. The airplane was lost, but there were no injuries or fatalities among the passengers and crew.[1]

Of the 13 events in which the pilot put the aircraft down in one piece, only to lose people afterward, the first occurred on November 29, 1938. This was a United Airlines DC-3 on a scheduled flight from Medford, Oregon to Oakland when it ran out of fuel. After impact the four passengers and three crew members immediately climbed to the top of the aircraft through the emergency hatch in the pilot's cockpit while the aircraft rode the swells easily until the surf carried it toward shore. However, of the seven people on board only one passenger and the pilot were still alive when help arrived.[2]

The causes of these ditchings, loss of an engine and running out of fuel, are only two reasons why aircraft have been forced to come down over water. Other causes include bad weather, faulty navigation, and in one case, a hijacking.

No mater what the cause, a successful ditching is based on many factors in addition to the pilot's flying skills. Among these factors are the angle of approach to the water, correct airspeed, liferaft location, emergency evacuation procedures, and breakaway engine design. All these were learned through trial and error, by careful experimentation, or as the result of aircraft evolution from propeller power to jets over the previous seventy years.

Part of the technology involved the evolution of long range aircraft. Initially these were flying boats designed to take off and land exclusively on water. This design was partly dictated by the lack of land-based aerodromes and airports capable of handling large aircraft as well as engineering design limitations of aircraft structure, and engines of the era.

Transoceanic flying was once an elegant experience. Passengers enjoyed amenities which rivaled those enjoyed by First Class passengers on the finest ocean liners or in a Five Star hotel. This past era of more genteel travel is as an essential part of the story as are the technical developments that made such trips possible.

Another crucial factor in safely flying across the oceans was weather. We take for granted our access to immediate weather information anywhere in the world. However, it wasn't until the first weather satellite was launched on April 1, 1960, that meteorologists were able to get a clear picture of what was going on around the world. Until then, off shore weather reports were sent by surface ships and, from 1941 through 1977, by U.S. Coast Guard cutters manning ocean weather stations at strategic locations along major air routes in the Atlantic and Pacific oceans. Weather forecasting and forecasting techniques were the same as those used by ships' officers. For fast moving aircraft this was often more of an educated guess than a statement of fact.

As with weather information, aerial navigation relied on the same tried and true marine navigation techniques from an earlier time. Aerial charts, celestial observation, and dead reckoning skills needed to be honed to a fine edge for the pilots to hit their destination on the mark. This, too, changed with the advent of radio beacons and radio direction finding equipment, long range radio navigation systems, and early satellites. These later evolved into today's extremely accurate global positioning system (GPS). The Coast Guard cutters also provided a mid-flight reference point for transiting planes.

One part of transoceanic flying that hasn't changed is the risk of ditching beyond the range of search and rescue (SAR) forces. A third part of the Coast Guard's ocean weather station duties was to assist aircraft in the case of ditching.

Nineteen of the 21 ditchings in which the plane landed in one piece took place in the open ocean. In all but two instances they were too far from immediate help, resulting in casualties from hypothermia or drowning. The two successful ditchings occurred within a half mile of Coast Guard cutters that were manning one of the weather stations.

For over 36 years there was a special relationship between airline crews and the Coast Guardsmen on ocean station. As each plane passed overhead a member of the flight crew radioed all pertinent information regarding the flight to the cutter. Often the stewardesses were the ones who handled this duty. The sound of a woman's voice was a welcome change to the men in the midst of a long patrol.

Within this special relationship, two went even deeper. The most special was forged by USCGC *Bibb* and a Boeing 314 flying boat named *Bermuda Sky Queen*. The other one was between USCGC *Pontchartrain* and a Pan American Airways Boeing 377 christened *Sovereign of the Skies*.

These two wonderful tales encompass many facets of ditchings: bad weather, engine failure, horrific sea conditions, and indomitable courage in the face of death. In addition to these two are stories of other ditchings as well as the journey we humans have undertaken from the beginning of transoceanic flight to today.

Now ladies and gentlemen, in preparation for take-off, please make sure your seat belt is securely fastened, turn off all electronic devices, sit back, relax, and enjoy the flight.

☙❧

2. Bermuda Sky Queen

"We did alright"

Chuck Martin

At 8:15 A.M. on October 14, 1947, Chuck Martin, the 26-year old pilot of the Boeing 314 flying boat *Bermuda Sky Queen*, attempted to do what had never been done before—land an 88,000 pound aircraft in 35-foot high seas. The lives of 68 passengers and crew on board depended on his ability. [3]

Manning Ocean Weather Station Charlie a mile away was the 327-foot US Coast Guard Cutter *George M. Bibb*. The cutter's crew watched as the plane descended. If it survived the landing, getting the passengers to safety would be their job.

The crew knew North Atlantic seas were powerful enough to beat a ship to death and they considered the chance of any aircraft surviving, even a ruggedly built Boeing flying boat, to be zero.

Word of the aircraft's distress was heard by other aircraft, and for the next 24 hours the world awaited news as the rescue unfolded. The drama was heightened when it was revealed the flight was no ordinary crossing. It was a charter flight with 62 passengers aboard, including women and children, and a crew of seven, the largest number of persons ever carried across the Atlantic in one airplane. A full load for a transatlantic flight in those days was only 21 passengers.

News of the impending disaster was picked up by the news-hungry papers in the United States and England. One headline read:

**Bermuda Sky Queen—Giant Flying Boat Down
In Atlantic with 69 Aboard!**

Prelude

When they were built in the late 1930s, the Boeing 314 was the largest commercial aircraft in the world. The comfort and luxury of the flying experience rivaled that of the finest ocean liners. The aircraft was 106 feet long with a wingspan of 157 feet—the largest wingspan of any commercial aircraft until the Boeing 747 exceeded it by only 38 feet. Powered by four 1,600-hoursepower engines, the 314 could carry up to 74 passengers, a crew of 10, and 5,000 pounds of luggage and cargo.

From the outside two irregular rows of big rectangular windows marked the upper and lower decks of the Clipper. Unlike the typical rows of seats in most passenger aircraft, the passenger deck was laid out as a series of lounges with couches on the lower deck. Sleeping berths, luxurious lavatories, silver goblets, and hot meals on real china served by white-coated stewards were all part of the hospitality Pan Am offered its passengers. On the upper deck were the flight cabin and baggage holds.

In early October, 1947, with American Airlines on strike, American International Airlines (AIA) contracted the *Bermuda Sky Queen*, to London-based Air Liaison, Ltd., to fly English emigrants and a number of British delegation employees to New York and the United Nations. The *Queen* had been reconditioned and furnished with regular seats in place of her more luxurious pre-war accommodations. She was taken from Floyd Bennet Field in July and flown to the British Overseas Airways Corporation (BOAC) base in Baltimore, hauled out of the water and inspected.

On October 2, she was flown back to New York and landed on the Hudson River off 79th Street in view of awe-struck thousands. Six days later the flying boat departed for Poole, England, under the command of 26-year-old Captain Charles M. Martin. Martin had flown 2,000 hours, most of which were logged in the US Navy PBY amphibian and PBM flying boat aircraft during World War II. The 2,000 hours included 162 hours in Boeing 314s. He was checked out for a commercial air license with single and multi-engine land and seaplane instrument ratings, was a certified celestial navigator, and a consummate sailor.

Martin's copilot was 34-year-old First Officer Addison Thompson. Addison held the same rank status as Martin and had accumulated 8,000 air hours, 102 of which were in 314s. The rest of the seven man flight crew were Second Officer Jack Sharer, First Engineer Walter Yaramishyn, Assistant Engineer Robert Hamilton, Radio Officer Willard Keith Woodmansee (an experienced Merchant Marine Radio Officer), and Steward Charles Penn.

This was Keith Woodmansee's second trip working for AIA. He'd taken the job while waiting for his ship *Yugoslavia Victory* to be repaired. His memories are quite clear as to what led him to the offices of AIA. " During this waiting period in New York, I found myself one day in the 16th floor shoebox office of an alleged attorney, whom we shall call 'Joe Shyster,' who represented an alleged 'charter' airline that needed a radio operator for a return flight to England. Back in four days. One hundred and twenty five frogs. 'Nuff said.

"This first trip proved the, shall we say, 'informal' nature of American International Airlines(!), especially the incident in which the skipper found it necessary to take up a collection among the crew to pay the $125 landing fee for setting down in Gander Lake.

"But after discharging our passengers from England at 69th Street, Hudson River, getting a good night's sleep and collecting the promised amount of Mr. Morgenthau's cabbage, I forgot the twenty six hours continuous radio watch (minus two hours gassing [refueling] at Gander), and decided to make one more trip in the lumbering old Boeing, garner the fast buck and be back in plenty of time to sign articles when the *Yugoslavia Victory* was ready to sail. Silly boy."[4]

When the *Bermuda Sky Queen* took off from the Hudson River for its North Atlantic flight to England, its engines made so much noise that the New York Police Department called AIA headquarters and demanded that the airline not bring the aircraft into the area again, there had been too many public complaints.

Three days later, Sunday afternoon October 12, Martin landed the *Queen* at Poole, England, and took on board her first passengers and their luggage. The plane's aft suite had been remodeled into a standard passenger compartment with seats. Many who stepped aboard recalled the 314s and their fame with Pan Am. An account reported some of the passengers were excited and thrilled to learn they were flying on a former Clipper.

Nine of those who embarked were U.S. and Canadian merchant seamen, homeward-bound after delivering the World War II surplus T-2 tanker *Chisholm Trail* to an English firm. Another contingent consisted of United Nations personnel returning from a conference in Geneva. Among them were Edgar and Gwen Ritchie along with their three-and-a half year old son Gordon. Gwen Ritchie wryly recalls: "We discovered to our dismay that they had added two very drunken Merchant seamen to the passenger list. They were flying back to N.Y. to pick up yet another newly built ship and deliver it to Europe. We had no idea our lives would probably depend on them and we would thank God for them."[5]

Into the Wind

After picking up passengers in Poole, England, the *Bermuda Sky Queen* landed at Foynes, Northern Ireland to refuel and pick up more passengers. Once in Foynes, the flight was delayed for over a day while the crew waited for the weather to improve. It was 3:40 P.M., October 13, when the *Bermuda Sky Queen* took off from Foynes and headed for New York. Her first scheduled stop was to refuel 1,730 miles away in Gander, Newfoundland, with an estimated flying time of 16 hours and 58 minutes.

Easterly head winds of 26 knots (35-miles per hour) were predicted so Martin loaded enough fuel to last 22 hours, a five hour margin of safety.

While in Poole, British Overseas Airways Corporation ground personnel told Keith Woodmansee that Boeings were never flown across the North Atlantic after October first and that Boeings never carried more than 40 passengers. The *Queen* would be carrying 62.

Reaching her cruising altitude of eight thousand feet and an estimated air speed of approximately 130 knots, *Bermuda Sky Queen* had clear skies for the first six hours.

First Officer Thompson assisted Shafer in taking the first celestial observation fix when the stars began to show their twinkle and just before an overcast blacked out the sky at 9:30 P.M. Before leaving his post for off-duty time, Thompson told Martin they would pass Ocean Staion Charlie, a U.S. Coast Guard weather station ship positioned 809 miles south east of Argentia, Newfoundland, at 2:00 A.M.. Calculations had placed the *Bermuda Sky Queen* 45 minutes behind schedule before reaching Ocean Station Charlie, 961 miles west of Foynes.

As the *Queen* slogged her way west, clouds appeared and ice built up on the wings. Martin tried to shake the ice off at 10,000 feet, then decreased the altitude to eight thousand and then to six. Ice from the four props spun-off, hitting the wings and fuselage and sounding like king-sized hailstones on a tin roof. Because the *Queen* did not have a pressurized cabin, Martin was limited to flying at or below 10,000 feet. Above that altitude there was not enough oxygen for the passengers to survive for long.

More dangerous than the ice were clouds hiding the stars, preventing Martin or Thompson from being able to fix their position. They had no way of knowing how strong the headwinds were.

Woodmansee remembers: "Halfway across on this last return trip, we passed over weather ship "Charlie" practically on our ETA, about ten hours out of Foynes, Ireland. Routine droning along at 6,000, trying to stay awake, sending routine hourly position reports to Shannon and VOAC [Gander Air Traffic Control]. Then, about fifteen minutes west of "Charlie," the stuff hit the fan, as they say in the crew's mess.

"At which time dumb Sparks learned that old Lady North Atlantic can be just as nasty in the upper air as on the tossing surface during the month of October. First came the soup. No visibility, consequently no celestial sights, for six hours. Atmospherics had the kibosh on the RDF gear. No LORAN."

When Martin and Thompson finally did get a celestial fix, the news was bad. Groundspeed for the six hours in the clouds had been 55 knots. Unknown to the crew the headwinds increased to 45 knots. The changes in altitude to shake off the ice burned more fuel than expected and, with the increased winds, *Bermuda Sky Queen's* margin of safety had disappeared. The only hope was to go back east to the waiting cutter.

Martin recalls: "I discussed the options with the other crew members. If we continued west, we might make the Newfoundland coast. Based on information from Gander we knew there were no ships in the area that could help if we ditched.

"I was sure a lot of people weren't going to make it," says Martin. His only hope was that anyone who did could endure the 50 degree water long enough to be rescued.

Keith Woodmansee was unable to reach the air traffic control center at Moncton, New Brunswick to alert them to the emergency. However, the *Bibb* was different.

"I'd always wondered if continuous watches were actually maintained on 8280 KCS, as indicated in the publications, and this stormy morning over the North Atlantic was a good time to find out.

"After sending this 'Urgent' to Nan Mike Mike Charlie [NMMC], the Coast Guard Cutter *Bibb*, on station at 45N 30W, I flipped the monitor switch to 'Both Receivers' to guard 6577, the regular guard frequency, and prepared for a wait on 8280.

"But that cutter was right on the ball—no more than a minute elapsed before a clean train of code shot out of the small Bendix aircraft receiver: KHFOG de NMMC QRK K[6]

"Ad Thompson, the pilot navigator, had just given me a position, so I shot this to Ocean Station Charlie just in case and then sent the rest of the message:

NC. 18612 QAB VOAC INSUFFICIENT FUEL-RETURN-
ING TO NMMC FOR EMERGENCY LANDING AT SEA. 62 PAS-
SENGERS 7 CREW, . . QSW 4220 A3 8280 CW"[7]

Passing near the *Bermuda Sky Queen* was a DC-4 cargo plane
that intercepted the distress call. Three-hundred miles eastward another BOAC DC-4 also picked up the urgent call. Homing in, both
planes joined the *Queen* as she headed east.

The cargo plane rendezvoused with the *Queen,* accompanying
her while the BOAC plane turned west to help locate *Bibb.* Two U.S.
Coast Guard Catalina aircraft carrying life rafts and survival equipment were dispatched from the Naval Air Station in Argentia, Newfoundland, to assist if the *Queen* had to ditch before reaching the cutter.

Radio traffic alert signals went out first to Halifax, then to
Coast Guard stations in New York, Boston, Newfoundland, and Canadian ports as well as to all North Atlantic shipping lanes. The passenger plane's radio operator notified the *Bibb* at 6:47 A.M. that Martin
would execute an emergency landing near the ship at about 8:00 A.M.

Semper Paratus

On board the *Bibb,* Radioman Second Class Ben White received
the radio message from the *Queen* stating the plane was headed toward
the cutter to ditch. Captain Paul B. Cronk, *Bibb*'s commanding officer,
was awakened by the duty messenger with the news.

Cronk had just fallen asleep after spending many hours at watch
when he was awakened by his quartermaster and told of the *Queen*'s
plight. On edge, and sounding grumpy over the lack of sleep, Cronk
told the seaman to order the preparation of rescue gear and to have his
steward brew up some coffee. He then fell back to sleep.

At 7:30 A.M. the plane was again contacted. Cronk was awakened and ordered that all rescue stations be manned. Still groggy, he
could hardly believe it when told that 69 persons were aboard the
troubled plane. He later remarked that he couldn't comprehend a passenger plane to be large enough to carry such a high number of people.

The biggest plane he knew about was the 42 passenger DC-4. Puzzled, stunned and still sleepy eyed, Cronk dressed and went out on deck.

"I found myself standing in the cabin, numb with shock." Cronk wrote later. "Where, in the name of Peace, had a plane with sixty-nine passengers come from? Transatlantic planes carried twenty-one passengers—the big ones forty-two. In my mind's eye I saw that flying eggshell collapse as it struck the sea."

Others on board reacted differently. Twenty-six year old Lieutenant junior grade (LTjg) Mike Hall, in charge of the Deck Department, reacted more forcefully. "You're shitting me!" he exclaimed. Hall was a seven-year Coast Guard veteran and, during World War II, became the first man to board an enemy warship on the high seas since the War of 1812.

Hall along with *Bibb*'s Navigation Officer Bernard S. Brown, Captain Cronk and others worked out plans to cover every contingency. Along with their own experience in Search and Rescue, they studied information compiled by the Coast Guard aviator Captain Donald A. MacDiarmid who initiated a multi-year study of open sea landing procedures in 1945. MacDiarmid's tests showed that landing and taking off parallel to the swell was the safest course. Despite all of the collective expertise, no one had ever faced such a massive sea-air rescue situation before.

Over the previous two days the winds had shifted from west to southwest, building up short, sharp cross seas with 30 foot high waves with only 200 feet between crests. In these conditions, the 327-foot long cutter rolled 80 degrees from port to starboard. The *Queen*'s wingspan was 152 feet, which left very little room between crests for her to maneuver.

As rescue plans were discussed, the crew began their preparations. Designated swimmers donned protective rubber suits, face masks and flippers; nets were draped over the side; and lifeboats were swung out, ready for lowering.

Regardless of the weather or sea conditions while on station, Mike Hall held daily boat drills. These involved launching and recovery of *Bibb*'s life boats, most of which were still powered by oars. Confident in Hall and in their own skills, the boat crews did not fear being sent out in rough seas.

The *Bibb* was no stranger to rescue work both in peacetime and during World War II, saving 301 survivors of torpedoed ships and providing an anti-submarine screen for other rescue vessels. In just one day she saved 235 lives. It was February 7, 1943, when *Bibb*, with Commander Roy L. Raney, USCG, as her captain, began taking aboard survivors of the troopship SS *Henry S. Mallory*, torpedoed during the previous night. In heavy, near-freezing seas the crew was taxed to the limit of their skills and strength. Because of heavy seas, only two or three rafts could be seen at a time; and some men wounded by the explosion had already died on the rafts.

Rescue operations continued with feverish pace throughout the morning during which time 202 survivors were taken from lifeboats and rafts. The same afternoon 33 additional survivors from the Greek SS *Kalliopi* were brought aboard. This date was a record day for rescue work at sea.

Down the Swell

As the *Bermuda Sky Queen* headed east in the early hours of October 14, no one on board was fully aware of the situation. Gwen Ritchie tells what went on.

"We slept fitfully in our seats—the sky began to lighten—there was the sun rising out of our starboard window! Almost home!——then suddenly we realized that it was coming up in the East and we were meant to be flying West. The word was whispered around as we shook ourselves awake and tried to make sense of this fact. Eventually a pilot cheerfully explained to us that as we were too heavily laden to fly high enough to escape the ice which was coating our wings, we had had to use up too much fuel to make it to New York and so we were going to come down at the nearest landfall. Not to worry!

"Soon after, we were told that in a little while we would look down and see the *Queen Elizabeth* heading for New York. They were going to take us on board for the rest of the journey. We would land beside them. Next we were told that the ship we could see below us was the USS *Bibb*. This was true. They said we would come down beside it and be taken aboard.

"Another Coast Guard cutter was racing from New York to take its place and the USS *Bibb* would then take us to New York. We didn't ask what fate they had planned for the flying boat. We knew instinctively we were being fed a lot of misinformation to keep us from panicking. So we all sat silently. Fear sat with us. Nobody spoke—not even the children."

Another passenger was Lillian "Tina" Lewin who recalls hearing about the impending ditching: "What amazed me most was the absolute lack of panic. The steward announced, 'You'd better break up your card game because we're going down to get a weather report.' We thought it was odd, but everyone just sat there calmly."

Shortly before 8:00 A.M. the *Queen* broke free of the low-hanging clouds. *Bibb*'s lookouts saw three small specks and soon recognized them as the *Queen* and her two land-plane companions. Three minutes later Martin swept over the cutter. Cronk and his men couldn't believe their eyes—they were stunned by the plane's size compared to the two smaller and circling DC-4s.

Now in voice communications, Chuck Martin discussed surface conditions with Cronk. It was the worst possible surface with no sea slope between the sharp crests long enough for the plane to skim and gradually settle in.

Strong winds whipped the sea's surface into 35 foot waves with the wind shredding the crests of foam. Cronk and his crew visualized the possible outcome and the horror of it all—when the powerful waves, acting like walls of stone, would tear the *Queen* to bits upon impact. Already some of the *Bibb*'s men stood poised to dive in for any attempted rescue—a deadly choice if undertaken in a wild ocean.

Cronk left the bridge wing and stepped inside the chart room where he talked to Chuck Martin who continued to circle above the boat. Wind direction and lengths of waves were noted. To have Martin skim over the wave tops and settle in was to ask for a miracle. Cronk suggested that the *Bibb* could calm the sea down a bit by circling, thus enabling Martin to nestle in the plane within the circled area. Martin, however, preferred to find his own niche. Despite Cronk's offer of assistance, Martin radioed: "I'll just pick out a spot and set her down."

For 20 minutes, Martin surveyed the waves. A calm spot was soon spotted and Martin, in a matter-of-fact tone, radioed he was coming down. Banking, the *Queen* glided seaward. Near the crest of a huge wave the plane shot up and circled again. Passengers, unaware of the landing danger, remained calm.

"The way they taught us to land was down-wind and across the swells, but I knew that approach wasn't going to work because high winds on my tail would make the aircraft too hard to handle and the landing speed too fast," Martin recalls. "So I planned to turn into the wind and watched for my chance to touch down on the backside of a swell."

Impact

Throttling down, he turned into the 35 knot wind and began descending. As a wave crest passed underneath, he chopped the throttles and pulled up into a stall, which instantly dropped the aircraft into the waiting sea. *Bermuda Sky Queen* touched down perfectly, but the relief was short–lived. The *Queen* slid down into a trough so deep it hid her from view. As she started to rise, the next wave smothered her under tons of water.

"Edgar and I were sitting next to the window," Gwen Ritchie wrote. "Looking out we could see what appeared to be a rock with white waves breaking over it. As we descended we could see it looked like a war ship. Closer down we could see that we were descending into a huge storm! It turned out to be a Number. 8 storm with forty foot waves. If it hadn't been for the incredible skill of those pilots the story would end right here.

"As was explained to us later, they came in for a landing on top of those enormous cresting waves and pulled back up for another go round—planning to land as close as possible to the cutter. We watched in horror at not just the height of the waves and the howling gale whipping the tops off them—but more so at the endless depth of the troughs in between. I am foolishly unafraid of water—I have always been unsinkable—but I was terrified. Around we came again and this time they managed to touch the top of a wave, skip to the crest of the next one and go with it—<u>down</u> into the trough, up the other side, a split second on the crest, <u>down</u> into the depths of the trough, up the other side——Well we had landed! We were floating! A slight misjudgment and we would all have kept on going to the bottom! A long way down!"

Woodmansee, used to rough weather, thought the landing went well.

"A couple of passes, a 'good luck' from the *Bibb*'s skipper on 4220 phone, and we strapped and braced ourselves in, while Charlie Penn, the Steward, did the same with the passengers on the deck below. Then, after saying our beads, praying to Allah, rubbing rabbit's feet, loosening emergency exit hatches, and swearing never to leave the ground again, we stopped breathing and sweated out the landing.

"Clunk! (first swell), Clunk! (second swell), and that's all there was to it (except for the next thirty-odd hours riding up and down). Old Chuck Martin (26 years) had set her down like a seagull dropping down in a tanker's wake for supper. No strain, no pain. Untangling ourselves from the pudding of overcoats, lifejackets and cushions, and getting up off the deck, we felt a bit sheepish for all the preparation."

Motor Machinist Mate Third Class Philips "Phil" Taylor was standing on *Bibb*'s deck when the *Bermuda Sky Queen* dropped under the clouds.

"Standing on the pitching deck, the huge four engine, forty–two ton *Sky Queen* was visible around a thousand feet or so as he circled the plane around us, looking for that spot to put her down, then she was down! He seemed to have picked out a large crest of a wave and went into a stall and dropped the aircraft on the wave."[8]

Miraculously the Queen emerged undamaged. Martin restarted the engines and taxied upwind toward *Bibb*. As he approached, *Bibb*'s crew started paying out a six-inch line kept afloat with kapok life-jackets.

The plane approached amidships and Martin stopped the engines about a hundred feet from the ship. As soon as the eddying effect of the ship's lee was felt, the *Queen* went out of control and surfed toward the cutter

Phil Taylor: "Suddenly, the distance between the aircraft and the cutter started to close. I moved to the fantail as I saw the starboard wing head for our mast and stack and the port wing going in the direction of our bow! Meanwhile, the *Bibb* was rolling some thirty degrees and as the plane moved towards us it was obvious that the cutter and the aircraft would collide. They did. As the plane's bow went down into a trough and started back up again, the cutter started her roll to port with the wing of the bridge coming down on the starboard bow of the airplane!!

"The cutter's propellers had started turning seconds earlier, but we could not pull away fast enough. I think some of our catwalk to the weather deck was damaged, as well as damage to the hull of the *Sky Queen*."

The plane's nose went down into a trough and started back up again, the cutter rolled to the left with the wing of the bridge coming down on the starboard bow of the airplane. Some of *Bibb*'s catwalk was damaged, but, more seriously, the *Queen*'s nose was pushed in and her two wing tips torn.

From inside the *Queen*, Gwen Ritchie had a different perspective: "It was quite a sight to see! The ships rails lined with sailors. Nearer and nearer and then CRUNCH!! as we slid into a trough, met the cutter, sliced off her railings and stuff on the starboard side—which damaged our wing and the nose of our aircraft and backed off (still going up forty feet and <u>down</u> forty feet with each wave). The cutter backed away too! The damaged wing was on our side of the aircraft. I expected it to break off any moment. The weight of the engine on the port side would just take us down into the icy depths."

Taylor narrowly missed being decapitated by a wildly swinging wing. With damaged wing tips and wounded nose, the *Queen* quickly drifted downwind.

You Have To Go Out

Within minutes Mike Hall and his crew launched a 10–oared Monomoy surf boat. In the heaving, foam-flecked sea it took constant pulling to outpace and circle the fast-drifting plane. Hall could not approach the plane from leeward where there was a danger of being surf-boarded under the fuselage.

Jutting out about 15 feet from each side of the plane's hull under the forward edge of the wings were mini-wings called sponsons to keep the plane from tipping over in the water. To Hall they looked like lethal weapons. Rising six feet or more above the water with the roll and pitch of the plane, they would slap down so hard that they could crush a small boat or swamp it with spray. Because of the heavy seas there was no safe way of coming alongside near the normal passengers' hatch in the plane's belly.

There was a hatch up near the plane's nose, but it was 20 feet above the surface at any time and lifting as high as 40 feet when a wave shot the nose upward. Anyone jumping into a wooden boat risked broken bones or worse.

As he studied the situation, Hall's instincts as a boat handler told him that it would be perilous to bring any manned or motored boat close enough to the plane to take people off directly. Quite apart from the thrashing sponsons, an approaching boat was threatened with being run down by the fast-drifting plane or surfing right into it as the *Queen* had done with *Bibb*. Such a collision would be no contest; the boat would be demolished.

Hall tried to reach the *Bibb* on his hand-held radio to share his conclusions with Captain Cronk, but he couldn't get through. They had been circling the plane for nearly an hour, and the men at the oars were tiring. Hall reasoned that Martin would have signaled him in some way if he felt that an emergency evacuation was in order. Hall headed back to *Bibb*.

If launching the Monomoy had been wild, retrieving it was wilder still. It brought about the first of several differences between Hall and his captain. Fearing for their safety, Cronk ordered all of the men out of the boat before hauling it up on the davits. Hall hesitated. He was in the stern, where he had been manning the sweep, and he was attaching the self-releasing hook on the falls from one of the davits. The hooks were designed to let go automatically as soon as the boat was waterborne unless they were secured with the proper turns of line. Hall thought that somebody should be standing by both stern and bow falls, but the others obeyed orders and scrambled out up the nets. Cronk yelled down, "Get out of that boat, Mr. Hall. I'm ordering you out."

Hall still balked. A knot of men at each davit was already straining against the falls, and the Monomoy was rising under him. Suddenly a wave lifted the boat and relieved the tension on the falls. The bow hook released; the boat hung precariously by the stern. Hall managed to scramble forward and re-hook the other fall. He was carried to deck level aboard the boat.

Having failed in two attempts to rescue people, another method had to be found.

No Easy Way Out

The air inside the tightly sealed plane became foul with the stench of vomit and fear. There was little food or water. Most of the passengers remained calm, but one woman was completely hysterical and had to be subdued, mainly by pouring gin down her throat. Others were screaming, falling down, or crawling as the plane rode the heaving seas. The plane's fuselage began to crack and rivets could be heard popping by everyone in the passenger compartments. Tina Lewin has other memories: "Louie and Scotty of the *Chisholm Trail* were about the only ones on the plane not sick. They were angels. They were wiping the children's faces, making them drink water, cleaning up the mess on their clothes, and helping them tear up sheets to wipe their faces and put around their necks and inside jackets. What amazed me most was the absolute lack of panic. Scotty was in some other compartment, but they were all moving around in all the compartments trying to keep things clean."

After the pulling boat failed to reach the plane, Martin and Cronk discussed using the *Queen*'s five-person life rafts, but when they tried launching a raft it flew like a kite or flapped about crazily in the sea.

Over the radio Martin could be heard retching, nevertheless he remained poised and calm. Attempts to launch life rafts from *Bibb* also failed due to the high wind.

Martin radioed that the plane was leaking, the sponsons were doubtful, and the tail was working loose. No one could know if or when a sponson would give way capsizing the plane or if a panicking passenger would open one of the many escape doors and flood the cabin. Less uncertain was the fate of the very young and the very old. They would not survive the night.

Hall and Martin agreed to try the rafts again. Martin suggested that only three men should make this first attempt using one of the *Queen*'s five-man rafts. The only safe exit was located on the left side forward of the passenger compartment and high enough so there was little danger of water getting in and flooding the plane. Three of the merchant seamen swiftly dropped from the hatchway door into the raft and paddled across more than a mile of open ocean.

Again, Gwen Ritchie takes up the story.

"The gale was blowing us along and we had no power now. Our electrical system had failed. They worked for hours on the system with intermittent luck. It was necessary to have it in order to keep our nose pointed into the waves. It seemed hopeless!! That's where those blessed, much maligned merchant seamen turned into heroes.

"Suddenly we saw a hatch open and out of it sprang two of the seamen wearing lifejackets and holding on to a small rubber raft! The hatch closed and we could see the sailors, holding fast to the raft being blown like a piece of flotsam, over and over, now right side up, now upside down, from crest to crest and finally they climbed into it, never letting go for a second as the wind tore at them, and with them inside it, it was blown straight towards the *Bibb*.

"By now the *Bibb* had a rope net hanging down its side with sailors hanging onto it. When the raft was flung up against it they grabbed the seamen and helped them up and onto the deck. We cheered and cried and wondered how this would affect us. We were told later that they, the seamen, had realized that with no food or water or any amenities including heat and with sixteen children on board, we would not be able to endure the gale and survive without the intervention of the Coast Guard cutter."

It was 3:59 P.M. by the time the three men from the first raft were safely on board *Bibb*. They were: Thomas R. Quinn, the chief officer, Arthur Brown, and Gerald Harmon.

"We were scared to death, I'll tell you," Quinn confessed. "We really didn't think we would make it once we were out there. And, I didn't know whether those women and children could make it."

Quinn had a good point: this method might work for men in good physical condition, but it would be too difficult for women and children. It took good balance and coordination to drop from the plane into the small raft as it swiftly rose and fell in the heavy seas. With winds blowing at 35 to 40 knots, air and water temperatures around 50 degrees, there was a very real possibility the children, and even some of the adults, could die from the complications of fear, shock, hypothermia, or exertion.

In addition, it had taken 17 minutes to transfer three people and there were only 93 more minutes until sunset. Twenty-three trips to transport 66 people would take more than six hours, if everything went smoothly.

Nevertheless, the merchant seamen's act of courage wasn't a waste. It proved a raft could be used in some fashion, and the *Bibb*'s crew learned to position their ship and lay down an oil slick to smooth the breaking seas when the *Queen* drifted into it.

A Perilous Leap

Through the day the cloud cover had increased and it was more like dusk than mid-afternoon. Cronk invited Hall to join him and the other officers for a conference to decide how to proceed. Hall, a man of action, remembers feeling the conference was interminable. There were few alternatives. Hall's reconnaissance had proven the limitation of the use of boats, and the discussion turned again to the large, 15–person life rafts. Hall thought they were the only way to go, and he supported his argument with his experience, less than a year before, when serving on the cutter *Algonquin* out of Portland, Maine.

It had been a December day with conditions far more severe than those facing the *Bibb*. A northeaster with 70 knot winds was raging, and a four-barge tow trying to exit the end of the Cape Cod Canal was losing ground, in danger of breaking up in the sharp, steep seas building up in the shallow water. When *Algonquin* reached the scene she didn't dare go alongside; she and the barges would have torn each other apart. But something had to be done quickly—the fourth barge with four men aboard was sinking.

The *Algonquin*'s executive officer Bob Wilson proposed a solution to *Algonquin*'s Commanding Officer George Vladimirovich Stepanoff[9]: Get as close to the barge as possible, inflate a 15-person rubber raft, float it over to them on a line, pull them back when they got aboard. The raft would be flexible enough not to cause serious damage in collisions with either barge or cutter. Stepanoff, who began his sea-going career as an officer in the Russian Imperial Navy under Tsar Nicolas II, quickly agreed. They tried Wilson's plan, and it worked to save two lives before the barge sank.

"Why wouldn't that work here?" Hall argued.

Cronk remained doubtful, having seen the way the rafts behaved in their latest attempt. While the discussion was in progress, Martin used precious battery power to radio *Bibb*: "We're beginning to leak. The tail section's coming loose. The sponsons look as if they might break away. Everybody's sick as a dog. Isn't there some way you can get them off before dark, Captain?"

Time for discussion had run out.

Lacking any other suggestions, Cronk decided to go along with Hall and sent down orders to inflate the 15-person rafts. Although the big raft gave them more favorable odds, the Coast Guardsmen were conscious that they had no time to waste, and the action aboard *Bibb* became, in Cronk's recollection, "fast and forlorn." When the crew lifted the first one over the side, his doubts about using the rafts seemed justified.

The first raft snagged on something, sprung a leak and deflated. The second's painter (the line from its bow) got caught in the *Bibb*'s starboard propeller and quickly wound itself around the shaft. Launched with more success, the third raft bobbed and scraped alongside with such force that it threatened to tear itself apart.

This nearly unmanageable movement suggested that the original idea of towing a raft back and forth between ship and plane as a shuttle was, at the very least, impractical. In a quick discussion among the officers, it was agreed to tow the raft to the plane, where it would be held as a loading platform, then drifted out on a line to a point where one of the *Bibb*'s small boats could approach and take the passengers off for delivery to the ship.

Again Hall volunteered to give this method a try using the ship's 26-foot motor surfboat. Designed to be used by life-saving stations on shore to get through heavy surf, its cockpit and deck were ringed by flotation tanks; its interior was honeycombed with air cells and packed with buoyant material. It was self bailing, which meant the hull was sealed off so any water that washed over onto the deck or into the cockpit flowed out again through ports for that purpose. Should the boat capsize, the crew could stand on the keel, grab the righting lines, lean back and rock it upright with their weight.

Made of wood, it weighed 5,800 pounds and couldn't be manhandled. It had to be swung out on davits and dropped into the water, no easy feat as *Bibb* was rolling almost 40 degrees to each side. With Hall were Bernard Brown, Chief Warrant Officer Lindall Hall (no relation to Mike Hall), Gunners Mate First Class John Johnston, and Chief Motor Machinist Mate Harry La Fever.

Once again disaster threatened. The boat's rudder shoe was knocked off when a roll of the ship banged it against the cradle. It had to be fixed. Ducking and dodging as the swinging hull took lethal swipes at their heads, the ship's carpenters repaired the damage, conscious all the while of a setting sun that was nearly touching the western horizon.

When the surfboat was in the water, Hall took the raft in tow and headed for the plane. It was a ride to test both the temper and skill of the boat's crew. In wind and waves, the light raft would surf madly along, threatening to ride right over the surfboat and its occupants. In the next moment it would pull away with such force that the light towline often broke. Hall would have to wheel around to catch and tether it again. No heavier line could be used for fear of tearing the fitting out of the raft's thin rubber walls. After a few time-consuming chases, Hall gave up trying to tow the raft and instead tied it alongside, where his four-man crew could help hold the bucking monster.

Back on *Bibb*, watching the raft nearly get away from the surfboat, a worried Cronk was considerably relieved when his men reported to the bridge that they had freed the second raft from the grasp of the propeller shaft and brought it back aboard.

Choices

On the *Queen*, hard choices had to be made in preparation for the arrival of the raft. Ordinarily, the rule of rescue at sea is women and children first. In this case, the all too evident risks and physical demands of the transfer process dictated a different procedure. As of that moment, nobody was injured or so acutely ill as to need the immediate medical attention available on *Bibb*. Yet everybody was weakened by seasickness and most where frightened.

The remaining six merchant seamen insisted on staying until the end to help with the others. As it turned out, their hardheaded strength came in handy when a number of people froze in the hatchway at the prospect of the long, uncertain leap and had to be thrown out forcibly. The rule settled upon was families would not be separated. As the passengers made ready to leave, it was discovered there were no child-size lifejackets on board. The younger children would go out in the arms of an adult.

Hall came as close to the plane as he dared and had the raft's painter passed across with a heaving line. The plane's crew hauled the raft in and tried to hold it under the nose hatch without letting it drift beneath the fuselage.

Woodmansee remembers: "We looked at it and wondered how in the hell we could get the women and children in that tossing rubber platform. For only seconds would it climb under the hatch, and then swiftly drop away again.

"After some difficulty, we drew the large raft up under the hatch. I hopped in, water up to my ankles in the raft, played the line back from the plane, and looked the situation over. With each wave, the raft would toss up and down, against the bow of the ship. From the raft, I didn't see how any women or kids would be able to get from the ship to raft, but people on the plane finally decided to try it."

Some of the passengers who were so sick on the plane said they would never be able to get to the door of the plane but it was most amazing. When action started they just brightened up and those who had been so helpless in the plane got into the raft.

William Bestwick, holding his 18 month-old daughter, Sandra, jumped next; his wife Josephine Bestwick followed, holding five-year-old Kenneth. Stewart Bestwick, aged nine, was considered old enough to make the jump himself with a little coaching. When a wave lifted the raft to within a few feet of the hatch, he was told to go, but he balked. Then, as it fell away, he jumped and missed. The men on the raft grabbed him and pulled him aboard. A spluttering Stewart said indignantly, "I'm ruining my good suit." Catherine Permet was the last to jump for that first load.

The Ritchies were also to be among the first load. "By the time we reached the broken nose of the plane (still pitching and rolling and going up and down forty-foot waves) two very frightened men had already jumped into the raft and taken Edgar and Gordon's places" Gwen Ritchie recalls. "I shall never forget their faces as they looked up at us like frightened animals afraid of being attacked. So full of fear—so full of shame!

"The ten year old and I were to jump together holding hands, but he pulled out of my grasp and leapt into the air towards the raft so far below us and only the incredible skill of the sailor in the raft saved him from going straight down into the watery depths! Then I jumped—I don't remember doing it. I don't remember being afraid!

"Then the father of the baby jumped with the infant in his arms and was settled down. I had never before seen a person with a really green complexion, but I was looking at one when the mother crouched at the edge and was unable to launch herself into the air in the direction of the raft—so someone gave her a little push. The little boy jumped fearlessly to join us and at that moment they decided that Edgar with Gordon in his arms would have to wait for the next raft. Their places had been taken.

"I have never known terror and desolation like those minutes as we pushed off leaving those beloved persons behind. I soon had to cope with the fact that the mother was incapable of looking after the baby. The father was in charge of both boys, the frightened interlopers were cowering at the bow—so I took the baby that was thrust into my arms—looking back at my own baby still on the plane. But Edgar was waving cheerily as if all was under control and soon I was too busy to worry. When we crashed up against the Captains boat we were unceremoniously hauled into it from the raft! They grabbed me by the hair—my arms were full with the baby—and just hauled us over the side of the boat! When we reached the Coast Guard cutter if looked HUGE!"

The plane's crew let out the raft's painter and Hall maneuvered the surfboat alongside, and his crew hoisted the passengers aboard. It was 5:30 P.M., two minutes before sunset.

When Hall reached the *Bibb*, he came in on the lee side, parallel to the cutter, and tried to hold steady while the cutter drifted down on him. As the boats converged, crewmen threw lines from *Bibb*'s deck to put around the passengers.

Other crewmen, soaked in cold spray, hung from the nets, reaching out to grab people with their hands. The roll of the ship was not measured, but the cutter's bell was ringing loudly and the roll had to be 38 degrees for the clapper to even touch the bell.

The surfboat crashed against *Bibb*'s side, tossing wildly up to the rail and down out of sight and, in the midst of it all, a baby was held aloft. Eager hands reached out for it. Phil Taylor remembers the scene differently than Gwen Ritchie.

"A woman in the boat, hysterically resisting attempts to place a line around her, screamed: 'Save my baby! Save my baby!' As the baby was snatched up by those on the nets and passed on board, she cried, 'Thank God, my baby is saved!'

So anxious was everyone to get the baby quickly on board the men got in each other's way. A hoarse voice shouted, "Let go, you stupid bastard! Are you trying to drown that baby?"

Once the baby was safely on board, one of the men held it aloft while running toward Sick Bay shouting: "I got the baby! I got the baby!"

Now the women were hauled on board. As they felt the deck, sensing their safety, they collapsed and were carried to sick bay. A pair of bearers picked up one of the women and attempted to carry her aft, only to fetch up short on the line still fastened to her.

"The plan had been for me merely to test the raft and get the women and kids in, but the insistence of the cutter's crew wouldn't allow me to go back to the plane, for which I was thankfully quite happy," recalls Woodmansee.

The first trip showed that survivors often needed assistance from the crew. On their own they either did the wrong things or did nothing at all to help. In the debarkation from the plane some needed to be thrown or pushed out of the hatch. In transferring them from raft to boat, the boat crew had to grab hold of them and heave. This operation was difficult because of the relative movements of boat and raft. When the first boatload of survivors came alongside, *Bibb's* regular rescue details were inadequate. Every man that could be brought to bear was necessary to bring helpless persons on board. And, at first, there were not nearly enough crewmen on hand to disperse the survivors once they were on board.

It was a hazardous situation for the men on deck, but, taking into account all phases of the operation, the men in the most danger of being injured were those on the scramble nets—they had to evade the boat which heaved up and down from deck to bilge level constantly.

Including the three merchantmen, there were now 10 of 69 plane occupants safely aboard the *Bibb*. Cronk radioed this good news to Boston for rebroadcast; the fate of the *Queen* had already become an international concern.

As darkness fell the wind picked up to 45 knots. In one sense, increased wind speed was a help. There was no time now for the *Bibb* to circle and spread oil downwind between rescue attempts, but it was discovered that the wind would carry the diesel oil down to the plane if the pump was speeded up, thus spouting the oil into the air.

Even so, waves broke through the slick and foamed into whitecaps, and Hall's next two trips, on which he ferried first 10 and then a dozen people, were as rough as the first. There were bruises as people jumped or were pushed from the plane and one man cut his head. But, nobody was seriously hurt and nobody was swept overboard as the operation went forward in the dark, relieved only by the cutter's searchlight.

Although Hall's seamanship was flawless, there was no way of taking the surfboat close enough to the *Bibb* to pass people safely to the rescue crews manning the nets without having it bump and bash against the ship's steel sides. Fenders that were normally used to keep ships from being damaged by grinding against other vessels or piers were totally useless that night because of the wide and different arcs through which the cutter and surfboat rolled. Wood is no match for steel in a collision, and how long the surfboat could withstand the punishment before being destroyed was anybody's guess.

The deck and cockpit of the boat were so constantly awash with boarding seas that it was hard to tell whether she was floating or not. Hall had to judge by feel and, by the third trip, he was worried: She felt limp and unresponsive. Obviously losing buoyancy, she was also running low on fuel. Hall had to risk more damage by tying up alongside the *Bibb* to refuel. It was torture for men and boat. While some of the crew tried to hold the boat off from smashing the *Bibb* with main force, the others went through the dizzy dance of pouring fuel into the tanks. With almost every wave crest, the boat was thrown against her restraining line at the bow with such a jolt that the crew went sprawling into the bilge.

"The boat was riding low in the water and responding sluggishly. I was reluctant to go back, but I knew people would be waiting for us," says Hall.

Once he had enough fuel Hall headed into the night to pick up the raft for the fourth time.

Adrift

Phil Taylor recalls what it was like: "While on engine room watch we were out straight with engine orders from the bridge. The *Bibb* was now in full swing using the fifteen-man raft and motor surfboat, and we were all joyous that the surfboat-raft procedure was the winning strategy in saving the people.

"Chief Warrant Officer Lindall Hall came down to the engine room after having made three trips with the motor surfboat. He looked pale and his leg had been injured. He relieved me on the throttles and ordered me to take his place in the surfboat. I went up to the port side and saw the surfboat in a semi-lowered position. I had a signaling light in my hand, jumped into the surfboat with Lieutenant Hall at the tiller, Lieutenant Brown and another crewman.. We grabbed the frapping lines for security as the deck crew let go the fore and aft lines. We were now afloat, scrambling to unhook the pelican hooks and follow the ship's searchlight into the darkness. I had the diesel engine at full throttle and Lieutenant Hall had all he could do to head into the wind and go to the *Queen.*"

Quite apart from increasing concern about the condition of his boat, Hall was finding each of these trips more worrisome. The plane's faster drift rate was gradually widening the distance from the *Bibb.* Martin did not dare to drain the plane's batteries by using lights, and she was only a faint gray ghost, appearing and disappearing as she rode the crest of waves into the far edge of the *Bibb*'s searchlight beam.

The distance put Hall out of communication with the *Bibb* except by Morse code flashed from a signal light he kept at his feet on the cockpit deck since his hand radio had been soaked and was out of commission.

As he drew near enough to see the plane in detail on the fourth trip, Hall had a severe shock. There was nothing that looked like a raft bobbing near her nose. He realized it must have broken its tether to the plane, and it would probably be loaded with people anticipating his return. Finding a black rubber raft playing hide-and-seek in the waves of a sea slicked over with black oil could be impossible. But Hall cruised slowly in the probable direction of a raft's drift and was soon able to home in on cries for help.

Reaching the raft, Hall got a second shock. It had evidently fared worse in collisions with the plane than his own boat had with the ship. One of the three flotation compartments was flat and airless. With 16 women on board, the raft was swamped and slowly sinking.

As fast as they could be hauled or pushed, the terrified people on the raft were tumbled aboard the already foundering surfboat. Hall could sense his boat sinking, and he shouted over the confusion, "Now hear me. Somebody's got to get back in that raft or we'll all sink. It'll only take a few of you and we'll keep you right alongside."

Three of Hall's crew volunteered and he sent them over to the raft. It was enough shift of weight to allow Hall to believe they could make it. In the overcrowded surfboat no lines could be found to secure the raft so men held it alongside with their hands. Hall opened the throttle to start moving upwind. There was a sickening, grinding noise. Hall knew at once a stray line from the raft was winding up in the propeller. Too late he threw the engine into reverse. There was a clunk and clatter as the gear box came apart under the strain of the fouled line. The universal joint on the shaft had snapped, so the propeller was useless.

Without power the boat broached and waves poured over the side. Women screamed and started instinctively moving away from the flooding water. Hall thought his boat would capsize and he yelled, "Stop! Stay still! Keep calm!"

The only hope for any of them was to maintain the balance of both boat and raft and somehow he managed to get that message across even though a number of women had reached the end of their control and gave in to hysterical weeping. Hall couldn't blame them. They were in real danger — with its buoyancy tanks about full of water and constantly swept by the sea, the boat was sinking.

Taylor recalls: "Lieutenant Hall tried to keep us all into the waves and save us from broaching. The sixteen women managed to stay together as we all clung to one another. I shouted to the group to hold onto each other and we would be picked up by the ship."

The *Bibb* lay a mile upwind. There was no way the men on its bridge could know Hall's plight. He fumbled for the signal light and asked people around him to search, but it couldn't be found in the tangle of bodies and wash of water. Without it, Hall could not let the cutter know what was going on as the rescued and rescuers drifted further from safety.

Hall made a megaphone of his hands and bellowed "Help! Help! Help!" into a wind that tore the sound away almost as soon as it left his lips. Futile as his gesture might be, he thought it would give the panicking passengers some sense of hope. In between shouts he kept reassuring them that, sooner or later, the ship would come find them.

From the wing of the *Bibb*'s bridge, Cronk and his engineering officer followed Hall's operation as well as they could. About all they could be sure of was that people seemed to be moving between the boat and raft. But the engineer didn't like the looks of things. "Neither of them seems to have much freeboard, Captain," he said.

"He's got a light. If he's in trouble, wouldn't he signal?" replied Cronk. Since *Bibb* was awkward to manage, Cronk was not anxious to close in on the small boat unless it became absolutely necessary. He asked several more officers to have a look. The consensus was, signal or no signal, Hall was in trouble. Cronk had the ship eased close enough to be heard through the bullhorn and called: "Are you all right? Acknowledge with your light."

When he heard that, Hall tried to yell back, but his answer was lost in the wind. It didn't matter. He and everybody with him knew at least they were not lost. Hall knew that retrieving them before their boat sank would require superb seamanship and a lot of luck.

Knowing the way things are likely to go during complicated rescues under adverse conditions, Hall was resigned to the probability that some lives would be lost. If his turned out to be one of them, he had already seen enough people safely across to make the sacrifice worthwhile.

He didn't share these thoughts. Instead he said, "Hear that? They'll fish us out before you know it. Just keep calm. Don't rock the boat. You up there in the bow on the right move in a little. Try to get a feel for the balance."

There was a moment of humor when one of the passengers sighted the *Bibb*'s white-hull: "You're a banana boat," she yelled. "You're United Fruit!" [United Fruit Company operated a fleet of ships to South America and all the ships where painted white].

By this time Hall did not have to spell out his predicament to the watchers on *Bibb*. If he had power, no seaman of Hall's ability would lay crosswind in these seas. If he had light, he would signal.

Cronk carefully maneuvered the *Bibb* into a position upwind of the boat from which, he calculated, she could drift down and bring them alongside at the scramble nets just aft of the bridge.

Everyone understood they might have only one quick chance to pull a person aboard before *Bibb* drifted over or past the helpless, sinking craft in which they huddled. Fortunately, Cronk landed the *Bibb* right alongside, but there was nothing more he could do as the boat and raft banged against the ship.

Tina Lewin wondered how she was ever going to get on board *Bibb*. "The raft was bobbing around and I tried to get hold of a line but it slipped through my fingers. After that I felt a terrific shock. I was in the water. Some woman tried to get hold of me, but I went under. Someone else got me by the scruff of the neck and got me back in. I thought that they'd strangle me if they pulled me up like that. Finally they got the line through one arm and then another arm. I was lying there, feeling pretty sick. Anyway, they pulled me up. They were just getting me over the rail and my dress was coming up and I kept trying to pull it down. One of the sailors said, 'Don't worry, lady, we're not looking.'"

The last passenger out was 60 year-old Mrs. Gloria Last. As she attempted to climb the nets, a swell pushed the hulls apart and she plunged between them. Boatswain's Mate First Class Ralph Keller saw her fall overboard between the boat and the *Bibb*. He dropped into the water, braced his feet and hands against the side of the *Bibb* and his back against the boat, saving Mrs. Last from being crushed.

Once on board, the women were taken to Sick Bay. Tina Lewis said in an interview later:

"I had a fur coat on. It was saturated. I felt pretty bad, but they got me undressed and gave me some long woolies and a jersey to put on but I couldn't get them on because I was all wet. And when I got them on they came along and said, "You'll have to take them off because they're all wet." And they took them all off again. I had some whisky, sugar and water and I got right up and have been up ever since."

Once again, incredibly, nobody was lost or badly hurt. The last person to stagger aboard the *Bibb* was Mike Hall, who went up to the bridge wing, saluted Captain Cronk and said, "Sir, may I have permission to take another boat and get the rest?"

Hall, who had gone into the water himself, was streaming wet. But, like the men on the nets, he had been too active and agitated to feel the cold. Not counting an earlier sortie in the pulling boat, Hall had been out on the water for more than two hours, but with his adrenaline up, his muscular body wasn't tired. He was resentful when Cronk denied his request.

A Long Night

After much abuse the surf boat was sinking; Cronk ordered it cut adrift to make room for other efforts. Cronk decided to send a Monomoy pulling boat with a raft in tow to the *Queen*. He called Ensign James Macdonald, who had shown some skill at handling the steering oar of a Monomoy during drills, and asked him if he would be willing to recruit volunteer oarsmen and try to get the last remaining raft to the plane.

Not only did Macdonald agree, but his call for volunteers over the loudspeaker system started a thudding drum of running feet as men hurried to the bridge. Macdonald had to resort to a first-come, first-picked basis of choice, weeding out those who had already had a turn in the boats. Chief Signalman Bunkley was taken along with a shoulder line throwing gun and a signal light.

Hearing the call down below Hall could only shake his head. More than anyone else aboard, Hall knew the dangerous odds they were facing. He had had the devil's own time dragging a raft down to the plane with the surfboat's motor going full blast. How could Macdonald do it with only six oars of a 10-oared boat being manned to leave room in the Monomoy to pick up people from the plane? Hall went back on deck to see if he could offer Macdonald any helpful advice and discovered others had been thinking along the same lines.

The plan was to take the *Bibb* a safe half mile downwind of the *Queen* and launch the raft and pulling boat there, spreading oil all the while. Macdonald and his oarsmen would simply try to hold the raft in position while the plane blew down on them.

The trick would be to stay out of its way, but be close enough to send the raft's painter to the plane with a shoulder gun. Hall still did not like the odds. He remembered the chilling sight of those thrashing sponsons. One error in the dark and the Monomoy would be smashed. Still, he gave Macdonald and his crew high marks for courage and he knew he would try it too, given the chance. It was what they were hired to do.

Launched at 11:39 P.M., Macdonald's boat towing the raft vanished into the darkness more completely than Hall's had. The black raft was almost invisible and the thin white hull of the pulling boat, flashing in the light beam only on crests, was often indistinguishable from the whitecaps rolling along in the same rhythm.

"It was very dark. Captain Cronk towed us on a sea painter to a position downwind of *BSQ* and considerably distant from same," Macdonald wrote later. "The *Bibb* illuminated the plane using the twenty-four-inch carbon arc searchlight. Wow, it was bright. Giving direction to the pulling boat with a sweep oar was erratic. I, therefore, used the oars to direct the boat—holding water on one side and giving way on the other—with raft to the BSQ.

"It appeared we might either hit the plane or miss it. Catching the drifting plane with the pulling boat would be impossible. When we passed close aboard to BSQ I had Bunkley fire a line over the bow cockpit of the plane. I could see that the plane crew had the line from the gun and were pulling on it."

The line landed on the left wing. In order to retrieve it Chuck Martin opened the hatch above the pilot's seat, pulled himself up on top of the spray-swept fuselage and crawled out onto the wing. Once he had the line, the painter attached to the raft was tied to the shot line and the raft was pulled alongside.

From *Bibb*'s bridge Hall and Cronk monitored Macdonald's progress as best they could. The plane's radio had gone dead, but Macdonald's voice occasionally squawked out of the darkness on the hand radio: "Passing *Queen*...Landed painter with third shot...Raft secured to plane...Awaiting passengers..."

A long silence followed, then: "No sign of action on plane..." More silence, then: "Still no action...No lights...Nothing."

Hearing this, Cronk and his officers were puzzled. The only conclusion they could reach, in the absence of any contact with Martin was that the 22 people still aboard the plane were too exhausted from 14 hours of plunging up and down, vomiting, and worrying to make the effort the transfer required. Cronk felt obliged to make sure there was no unimaginable problem on the *Queen*. Once Macdonald and his boat were safely aboard, Cronk took *Bibb* in close to the plane at 15 knots, to maintain control and hailed Martin through the bullhorn.

"How do you feel about spending the night on the plane?" he asked.

Using the plane's landing lights, Martin responded with: "Affirmative."

On *Bibb*'s bridge, it was agreed Martin had made a wise decision. Even if the plane sank they had the raft which was capable of supporting 25 people with 15 aboard and 10 hanging on the grab lines. The cutter could drift down and pick them up in minutes. Cronk sent half of his crew to their bunks and kept the other half on deck at Ready Stations for instant action.

Edgar Ritchie was one of the passengers remaining on board. Of that night his wife would write: "There were about 16 men and one woman, who probably out of fear, spent the night drinking and the last ten hours throwing up thus rendering the Ladies Room unusable. The woman refused to jump! No amount of cajoling to get her off as darkness fell and the men would not leave before she did. They chose to stay with her on the flying boat hoping for the storm to calm down when she could be less afraid to jump."

Everyone was exhausted. After sending his last message for the night, Martin finally relaxed and tried to get some sleep. The men played cards all night expecting not to survive, the woman slept, and the crew worked to keep the *Queen*'s nose into the waves.

Death of the Queen

When the sun rose at 6:45 A.M. on October 15, the gale had diminished to a fresh breeze and the seas had gone down. In the grey dawn two boats were launched to complete the rescue. James Macdonald was in charge of one and Phil Taylor had the other.

"I did take two more survivors on board," wrote Taylor. "One of which I noted had a brief case attached to his wrist. I thought he was probably a diplomat. I remember him for two reasons. As I pulled him on board, his body hit the control panel to the engine. The diesel engine stopped!! I did not realize what had happened, so I got busy checking the engine, only to hear the megaphone voice of Mr. Webb, the Chief Engineer.

"He was lambasting me for not checking the fuel, etc. Now I noted Captain Cronk had signal recall flags hoisted to get me to hurry up!! I did find the problem quickly. The diplomat had hit the shut off control solenoid that shut down the engine. Later I learned this man was the father of Gordon Ritchie, who was a four year old boy passenger rescued with his mother the previous day."

By 9:13 A.M., everyone from the *Queen* was on board the cutter, the boats secured, and the ordeal over. There was no way to save the valiant *Bermuda Sky Queen*. She had to be sunk; afloat she would be a menace to navigation.

Chuck Martin sadly watched as 20-millimeter bullets were fired into the *Queen*. The aircraft did not explode as the bullets penetrated her hull, but instead she caught fire. When *Bibb* departed the scene black smoke was visible, marking the grave.

Gordon Ritchie remembers his time on *Bibb*: "Once aboard, it did not take me long to recover. Indeed, I recall later that night being sternly admonished by one sailor that bad little boys were stuffed down a manhole which he proceeded to open. That kept me quiet for a bit."

Gwen Ritchie's memories are more vivid. "So we sailed for home! It took us four days and nights under very difficult conditions (for the crew of the Bibb as well!) After all a Coast Guard cutter is a small ship with a complete crew. We added 69 to their numbers! Sixty nine who needed beds and food and medical attention! Sixteen of them were children. The young sailors blew up meteorological balloons for them to play with because we were discouraged from going out on the decks—I imagine because the ship was travelling so fast and in such rough seas! We took group showers with the children. I imagine the men shared the remaining crew facilities with them! The bakers baked day and night! The medical facility was open all night and snowed under with requests for diapers and other necessary supplies for the ladies."

Return to Shore

With a broom tied to the mast (to indicate a 'clean sweep') *Bibb* triumphantly sailed into Boston Harbor and tied up at Constitution Wharf. There she was met by a band, Boston's Mayor James Michael Curley, and a dock full of people. Because it was Sunday and all stores were normally closed, Jordan Marsh and Filenes department stores opened their doors so the survivors could purchase clothing. The Red Cross had people there to help make flight and travel arrangements.

However, the weary and now wary Keith Woodmansee tells of a different side to the homecoming.

"Luckily there was no other news in the States at the time, and the papers palsied it up in their sensational and razzle-dazzle manner. I say 'luckily,' because if I hadn't been able to sell those photographs to the Daily News, I'd not have received one cent for that flight—"Joe Shyster" had drawn the "airline's" money out of the bank immediately upon hearing the plane was down, and declared bankruptcy in some. The 200 frogs [dollars] received from the News for my pictures just about covered my expenses and the gear I lost when the *'Queen'* was sunk by gunfire as a menace to navigation. As to the *Yugoslavia Victory*, my new-found 'home,' by the time we finally got back to the States on the cutter, she'd long since sailed for the West Coast.

Afterward

A testimonial to officers and crew was held in the main ballroom of the Copley Plaza on October 29. The speakers included Edward Foley, Assistant Secretary of the Treasury and Rear Admiral Merlin O'Neil, Assistant Commandant of the Coast Guard.

On November 12, Mike Hall and Ralph Keller received the Coast Guard Gold Life Saving Medal, the Coast Guard's highest peace-time award for heroism. LT (jg) Bernard Brown, Commander John N. Feller, Lieutenant Robert E. Webb, LT (jg) Lewis Francis (US Public Health Service) M.D., LT (jg) Raymond G. Parks, Ensign John W. Steffey, Chief Clemens H. Brendle were awarded the Silver Life Saving Medal for their part in the rescue. Captain Paul Cronk added a gold star to his Legion of Merit.

The Civil Aeronautics Board (the forerunner of the Federal Aviation Administration) and the Coast Guard begin investigations into the loss. Several of the passengers initiated lawsuits against American International Airways, owner of the *Bermuda Sky Queen* and Captain Martin as well as other members of the flight crew. Since all of the logs and records of the flight were on board the *Queen* when she sank, there is little hard evidence to go by.

Testimony from the passengers, flight crew and others resulted in Martin being fined $200 and American International Airways had its Letter of Registration (i.e. its permission to operate) suspended indefinitely and they were fined $500.[10]

When Chuck Martin and Mike Hall were asked how they felt about the rescue, Chuck's reply was: "We did alright."

Mike Hall said simply: "We were just doing our job."

Lessons Learned

Chuck Martin's ditching of the Bermuda Sky Queen wasn't widely studied by other pilots at the time. Perhaps this was because it was a flying boat and not one of the many land-based commercial aircraft being flown at the time. For whatever reason, his landing validated the ditching protocols developed over the previous 10 years.

The Coast Guard did examine the event closely and made several changes to the recommended Ditch and Rescue procedures used by ocean station ships. These changes had significant impact on all successive Coast Guard ditch and rescue operations.

3. Flying the Oceans

"I love to sail forbidden seas, and land on barbarous coasts."

Herman Melville, Moby Dick

Bermuda Sky Queen was the last of the great commercial flying boats. Her funeral pyre marked the end of the first brief era in transoceanic flight even as a second era was being born. This second era was destined to last for even less time, but its passing ushered in what is the third and longest lasting era of flight. Each era contains visionaries, brilliant innovations, and safer ways of traversing oceans.

The first era, from 1903 to 1945, spanned less than 50 years. Within that time aviation progressed from its first faltering steps to maturity, from men flying hand-built single engine aircraft capable of a few seconds of flight to multi-engine, propeller-driven behemoths able to span oceans.

Beginning in 1945 and ending in the mid 1950's, the second era was driven by increasingly powerful engines. Although enabling larger aircraft to fly further and faster, the complexity of these engines and the attendant propeller systems proved fatal for both planes and passengers in several ditchings.

The birth of the third era was heralded by roaring jet engines. It is an era of unparalleled safety. Although far safer than the other eras it, too, has seen several ditchings.

Let's look at how flying the oceans evolved from a dream to a luxurious adventure to an interlude on our way from one place to another. At the end of the chapter are two tales about the price in lives and aircraft along the way.

Birth of an Era

For untold millennia humans dreamed of breaking their earthly bonds to soar in the vast sky and over boundless seas. Making this dream a reality eluded our grasp until two American bicycle makers from Dayton, Ohio came along. It took them 12 seconds and 120 feet over an obscure North Carolina beach to set us free. They were the Wright Brothers, the date was Thursday, December 17, 1903 and the place was Kill Devil Hill, Kitty Hawk, North Carolina.

Wilbur and Orville Wright made the first of four sustained, powered flights under the control of a pilot on the morning of December 17, 1903. Over the next two years they continued their work in a pasture near Dayton, Ohio. Unwilling to unveil their technology without the protection of a patent and a contract for the sale of airplanes, the Wrights did not make public flights until 1908, at which point they emerged as the first great international heroes of the century.[11]

While the Wright brothers worked to improve their aircraft, men in Europe were also taking to the air. Among these was Louis Bleriot, a 37-year old French inventor, aircraft designer, and self-trained pilot. He flew across the treacherous English Channel early on July 25, 1909, in the Bleriot XI, an aircraft he designed himself. Bleriot braved adverse weather and 22 miles of forbidding sea in his flight from Les Barraques, France to Dover, England.

The generally-accepted father of the flying boat is Glenn Curtiss, who flew a series of seaplanes in 1911. In 1912 Curtiss produced the two-seat *Flying Fish*, a larger craft that became classified as a flying boat because the hull sat in the water. It featured an innovative notch (known as a 'step') in the hull for breaking clear of the water at takeoff. Curtiss correctly surmised that this configuration was more suited to building a larger long-distance craft that could operate from water and was also more stable when operating from a choppy surface. In 1914, collaborating with the retired English naval officer John Cyril Porte, Curtiss designed the *America,* a larger flying boat with two engines, for the Atlantic crossing. This effort stalled with the outbreak of war in Europe late that summer.

The Atlantic Challenge

Near the end of World War I, the Navy requested an aircraft that would be able to cross the Atlantic under its own power and go directly into action against the German U-boats which were sinking tons of merchant ships each week. Under a joint venture the Curtiss Company and the Navy designed and constructed large flying boat patrol aircraft.

On May 8, 1919, NC-1, -3, and -4 took off from Naval Air Station Rockaway in Long Island, New York, with Trepassey, Newfoundland, the intermediate stop prior to their attempt at the Atlantic. On May 16 they left for the longest leg of their journey, to the Azores, with 22 US Navy warships stationed at 50 mile intervals along the route. NC-1 and NC-3 were forced to land at sea due to rough weather. The crew of the NC-1 was rescued by the Greek freighter Ionia while the crew of the NC-3 managed to sail and taxi their flying-boat to the Azores.

The NC-4 reached Horta in the Azores on the following afternoon, having encountered thick fogbanks along the route. She was the first aircraft to cross the Atlantic.[12]

A month later British aviators John Alcock and Arthur Brown made the first non-stop transatlantic flight. Flying a modified World War I Vickers Vimy bomber they took off from Lester's Field in St. John's, Newfoundland at around 1:45 P.M., June 14, 1919. In poor visibility they misidentified a bog as a suitable grass field to land on and their aircraft technically crashed on landing in a bog near Clifden in Connemara, Ireland, at 8:40 A.M. on June 15, 1919.

It was more than five years before the next trans-Atlantic flight took place, this time from east to west. On January 22, 1926 Ramón Franco piloted the German-built Dornier twin-engine flying boat Plus Ultra from Huelva, Spain to Buenos Aires, Argentina. With stops at Gran Canaria, Cape Verde, Pernambuco, Rio de Janeiro and Montevideo the 6,400 mile journey took 59 hours and 39 minutes.

After the successful NC-4 and the Dornier trans-Atlantic flights, the growing commercial airline industry realized the huge potential in flying boats for long haul travel.[13]

Flying Boats

Prior to World War II, airports capable of handling large, long-range aircraft were few in number and nonexistent in most parts of the world, particularly in undeveloped nations. Most nations, however, are located near or encompass lakes, rivers, harbors, and inlets which required little if any development for the operation of large, long-range flying boats.

German development of long range flying boats led Short Brothers, a British aircraft firm, to build forty-two Short Brothers S23 C Empire Flying-Boats to service the globe-spanning British Empire in the late 1930's.

Airlines operated both passenger and freight service with flying boats, and the military used these aircraft for reconnaissance, antisubmarine patrol, search and rescue, and other activities. In addition, the flying boat seemed to offer the prospect of a safe landing in the event of an engine failure, a very real possibility with the relatively unreliable engines available in the early days of aviation.

At this point, US commercial airlines were slowly developing transcontinental air routes along with limited service to the Caribbean and South America. The British controlled the North Atlantic air routes, but no one had attempted to tackle the challenge of crossing the Pacific.

Flying over the Pacific presented a much greater challenge than crossing the Atlantic. The routes across the Atlantic were relatively short, and it was even possible to follow an extreme northern route where the longest over-water leg would be the 496 miles between Greenland and Iceland. Even the direct route from Newfoundland to Ireland, which avoided the harsh weather of the far north, was under 2,000 miles. But the distance from San Francisco to Honolulu was almost 2,400 miles. The next leg of the Pacific crossing from the cable station at Midway to the next inhabited island at Guam was even farther.

Juan Trippe, founder and president of Pan American Airlines, tackled the challenge of mastering the Pacific.

The Pacific Challenge—Juan Trippe and Pan American Airways

Not only did Pan Am have to deal with the problems of open ocean navigation, but also with the fact that no plane of the day had the needed range capability. Juan Trippe did notice, however, that Hawaii, Guam, and Manila formed a line of stepping stones to Asia. Further investigation revealed the islands of Midway and Wake breaking up the 4,000-mile expanse of ocean between Hawaii and Guam.

Trippe searched for a solution, and discovered a small, uninhabited Pacific island named Wake. Claimed by the United States in 1899, but deserted and virtually forgotten, Wake was 1,200 miles from Midway and within reach of Guam; the perfect stepping-stone to cross the Pacific.[14]

Trippe's success in developing Pacific air routes was due to his chief pilot, Edwin C. "Eddie" Musick, a veteran Navy flier. Musick flew ahead to stake out the best landing facilities, establish communication relays and weather stations, and plan the best routes and schedules. His contribution was acknowledged by Trippe to be the key to Pan Am's success in South America and the Pacific.[15]

Frederick Joseph "Fred" Noonan was the navigator on the first Pan Am Sikorsky S-42 clipper at San Francisco Bay. He navigated the historic round-trip China Clipper flight between San Francisco and Honolulu piloted by Ed Musick. Noonan mapped Pan Am's clipper routes across the Pacific Ocean, participating in many flights to Midway Island, Wake Island, Guam, the Philippines, and Hong Kong.[16]

Pan Am's pioneering survey flights were made using the Sikorsky S42. Having a range of only 1,200 miles, this four-engine flying boat was outfitted with extra fuel tanks to make the journey possible. Passenger service would not begin until Trippe received the first Martin M-130, which had a range of 3,200 miles and seating for 36 passengers. Starting on October 21, 1936, the M-130s were carrying passengers.

Once the distance problem had been solved, there still wasn't an aircraft capable of making the flights. To solve this one, Trippe worked closely with Igor Sikorsky in creating the S-40, the first of the "Clipper" flying boats.

He decided to call his flying boats clippers after the far-ranging type of sailing ships of the 19th century. This was part of his effort to link his airliner with the maritime heritage of the ocean liners with which Pan Am was competing. Trippe also came up with the concept of having his aircrews wear naval-style uniforms with gold ring naval ranks on the jacket sleeves. Along with the naval-style uniforms went the nautical titles of Captain, First Officer, Second Officer, and Purser. An added touch to the nautical theme was that during the flights, a ship's bell rang the hours.[17]

The first S-40, christened Caribbean Clipper by Mrs. Herbert Hoover in a ceremony on the Potomac River, began service in 1931 and was followed by the American Clipper. Although it could carry up to 40 passengers the S-40 lacked the range for Pacific operations. That requirement was met, initially, by the S-42 which carried up to 32 passengers with convertible sleeping accommodations for 14 of them.

Sikorsky S-42s were soon replaced by Martin M-130s. This airliner gave Pan Am the true ability to span the world's oceans. It could carry 46 passengers in daytime configuration, but in its more typical overnight service it provided sleeping accommodations for up to 30 passengers in three 10-berth compartments (one forward and three aft) with a 16-seat dining room/lounge compartment located amidships.

Passengers had all their needs catered to by the ever attentive stewards and food and drink was always available. A favorite drink served on the clippers was the Clipper Cocktail (1 ½ oz. light or gold rum, ½ oz. vermouth, ½ tsp. grenadine. Combine all ingredients and pour over cracked ice into chilled cocktail glass.).

Inaugurated with great fanfare, the China Clipper began the first commercial transpacific flight on November 23, 1935, departing from San Francisco and landing in Honolulu. Five days later it arrived in Manila, via Midway, Wake, and Guam.

Once the route was established, it became clear that a significant advancement in airplane design was required if commercial aviation was to be extended further. Boeing met this requirement with the grandest embodiment of flying boats ever created—the B-314, the largest commercial plane until the arrival of the Boeing 747 almost 30 years later.

The 314's were stately flying boats and the experience of travelling on one rivaled that of the ocean liners at that time. Sleeping berths, lounges, luxurious lavatories, silver goblets, hot meals on real china served by white-coated stewards, were all part of what Pan Am offered to its passengers. There was even a honeymoon suite.

On the outside were two irregular rows of big rectangular windows marking the upper and lower decks of the Clipper. The upper deck was made up of the flight cabin and the baggage holds.

Unlike the typical rows of seats in most passenger aircraft, the passenger deck was laid out as a series of lounges with couches. As one moved to the back of the plane, there were steps up into the next compartment due to the curvature of the bottom of the plane. The couches were made into beds at night. The main lounge was transformed into the dining room at mealtimes.

The European airlines, particularly BOAC, were hard pressed to keep up with the beautiful Boeings flown by Pan Am. England's Short Company continued to build the Empire, but could not compete when Pan Am finally turned its attention to the Atlantic routes.

Pan Am inaugurated the first US transatlantic mail service on May 20, 1939. Under the command of Captain A. E. LaPorte, almost a ton of mail was carried from Port Washington, New York to Marseilles, France via the Azores and Lisbon in 29 hours. The same aircraft, commanded by Captain Harold Gray, opened the northern mail service to Southampton, England on June 24, 1939.

Just over a month later the Dixie Clipper, under the command of Captain R.O.D. Sullivan, inaugurated Pan Am's first regular passenger service from New York to Southampton, England, via Gander, Newfoundland.

The golden age of the commercial flying-boats was abruptly interrupted by the outbreak of World War II on September 1, 1939.

The war curtailed Pan Am's opportunity to build on its success. The northern transatlantic route was abandoned after only three months, on October 3, 1939.

When the United States entered the war Pan Am sold the 314s to the US government and BOAC for over one million dollars each. All of the clippers saw war duty, but none was lost to enemy fire although they were fired upon more than once. An interesting side note is that the Pan Am crews were contracted by the Navy and continued flying their aircraft.

After the war the government offered to sell the US owned planes back to Pan Am for $50,000 each; Pan Am declined the offer. By that time flying boats were no longer efficient international carriers.

End of Flying Boats

The end of the flying boat airline era ended with World War II. The flying boats were designed because there were originally very few long runways able to handle a large airliner. Also, prior to WWII, land-based aircraft didn't have the range and load-carrying capability of the flying boats. The significant design changes brought about by the war negated these differences.

In late 1945, there was a large number of planes (mostly ex-bombers and transports) and lots of concrete runways on former military bases around the world. The combination of long-range land-based aircraft and the facilities to support them were the death knells for flying boats.

Also, the war shifted the gears of the country, making time a more important consideration than comfort. New technology and simple economics turned the attention to faster and more convenient land-based planes. Therefore, it was natural that the airlines restarted services with aircraft purchased cheaply from the US Army Air Force.

Second Era—Post World War II Commercial Aviation

Transatlantic air travel in the immediate postwar years remained a novelty, but it offered significant advantages over sea travel. Cooperation between Western European countries and the United States increased tourism and made air travel easier.

Pan Am, TWA, American Overseas (acquired by Pan Am in 1950), and Trans-Canada were the four North American pioneers of transatlantic air travel in the immediate postwar era. From the other side of the Atlantic, British Overseas Airways Corporation (BOAC), SAS, KLM, Air France, Sabena, and Swissair were all flying in this market by 1950. It was the heyday of the great propeller airliners.

The North Atlantic had the impetus of strong economic activity and cultural ties between North America and a reconstructing Europe. Driven by economic growth on both sides of the ocean, the North Atlantic soon became the world's most important and heavily traveled international air market.[18]

Transpacific air travel—this time with land planes—resumed in 1947 when Pan Am and Northwest Airlines both inaugurated Boeing 377 Stratocruiser services between North America and Asia via Tokyo. No airliner in the propeller era had sufficient range capability to fly nonstop between the United States and Japan, so a "technical stop" for refueling was required in Hawaii or Alaska.

Japan Airlines entered the transpacific market in 1954 with Douglas DC-6B services that linked Tokyo with San Francisco. JAL introduced the DC-7C "Seven Seas," the last of the propeller airliners, two years later.

At that time, only a half-dozen airlines in the world flew the Pacific, which was only just beginning to show hints of the tremendous growth that would occur as Japan rebuilt its powerhouse economy, traded with North America, and invested regionally to spur growth throughout Asia Pacific.

Over the decades, one of the most dramatic trends in commercial aviation has been the ongoing increase in airliner range capabilities. Because of the vast scale of the Pacific Ocean, airplane range has played a defining role in the evolution and development of transpacific flight operations.[19]

A number of new airlines were started by former Army and Navy fliers encouraged by the availability of inexpensive aircraft and the plethora of trained aircrews and maintenance personnel. Two of the better known were Transocean Air Lines and Flying Tiger Airlines.

In addition to using aircraft designed during WW II, airlines invested in newer planes, including the Boeing 377 Stratocruiser, Lockheed Super Constellation, and Douglas DC-6 and DC-7. These designs incorporated advances including aviation electronics (avionics), pressurized cabins, improved radio navigation aids (see the chapter on Navigation), high density seating, advanced propeller systems, and highly complex engines.

These last two advances, propeller systems and engines, stretched the design envelope, and proved problematic. Here are brief descriptions of the three aircraft then we'll look at the engines and props.

Following the tradition set by the 314, Boeing's Stratocruiser set the luxurious standard for air travel with its decorated extra-wide passenger cabin and gold-appointed dressing rooms. A circular staircase led to a lower-deck beverage lounge, and flight attendants prepared hot meals for 50 to 100 people in a state-of-the-art galley. As a sleeper, the Stratocruiser was equipped with 28 upper-and-lower bunk units for First Class passengers.

For sheer beauty few aircraft have ever matched Lockheed's Constellation's triple-tail design and dolphin-shaped fuselage. The four engines were set farther out on the longer wings, which meant less cabin noise. Noise was further reduced with state of the art sound deadening materials. Cabin temperature control and ventilation were perfected. Seats were fully reclining for comfort on long flights. Everything about the aircraft was impressive for its time and, except for the engines, it was practically a trouble-free aircraft.

Although more prosaic in appearance on the outside, the Douglas DC-7, featured leather seats and a first class smoking lounge.

Although among the most luxurious state-of-the art aircraft of their day, all three were plagued by engine and propeller troubles which proved fatal.

Stretching the Design Envelope—Engines and Props

Radial engines and the propeller systems evolved through the 1930s, but as with aircraft design, World War II accelerated the use of these systems. They are the systems which enabled larger aircraft to fly farther, faster, and carry more weight.

Engines

There are two options for arranging pistons in a engine. One is the in-line design which includes "V" engines found in most automobiles with the driveshaft at the bottom of the engine. The other design arranges cylinders in a circle or "radial" pattern around the drive shaft. Although radial engines are wider, the design allows for rows of seven or nine cylinders to be arranged front to back, dramatically increasing the available horsepower. This arrangement also increased the problems of engine cooling, reliability, and maintenance. Here, respectively, are the arrangements for the Boeing Stratocruiser, Lockheed Constellation, and Douglas DC-6 engines.

Stratocruisers used Pratt and Whitney R-4360 Wasp Major 28 engines. Each row of seven cylinders was slightly offset from the previous one, forming a semi-helical arrangement to facilitate efficient airflow cooling of the successive rows of cylinders. This helped with airflow and cooling, but this wasn't always successful.

Curtiss-Wright Cyclone 3350s powered the beautiful Constellation. The 18 cylinders were arranged in two rows. The Pratt and Whitney R-2800, two-row, 18-cylinder engine is still in service and considered one of the premier radial piston engines ever designed.

Although all three were well designed, tested, and built, each one suffered catastrophic failures in flight.

Propellers

When we think of propellers, the two-blade wooden one used in WWI comes to mind. This is as obsolete a concept as the planes that used them. From 1928 to present day the propellers on many multiengine aircraft are either variable (also referred to as controllable) pitch or constant speed designs.

With controllable or variable pitch propellers the blades can be rotated around their long axis to change the angle or pitch at which the blade bites into the air.

A constant speed propeller can change its blade pitch to take advantage of the power supplied by an engine in much the same way that a transmission in a car takes better advantage of its power source. The mechanism varies depending on the aircraft, but the desired effect is to change the angle of attack of the propeller blades to take a smaller or larger bite of air as it rotates.

Both types of propellers are controlled either electrically or by hydraulics which adds another layer of complexity to the aircraft's systems.

Troubles

Incidents of over-speeding engines and lost propellers plagued all aircraft. Most ditchings from 1947 through 1962 were the result of mechanical failures. With all radial engines there was a danger that an over-speeding engine would catch fire or turn so fast that the prop would spin off. At times the engines burned so hot they fell off the wing or the propeller was flung into the passenger compartment.

One such accident occurred on an Air France Latécoère 631 six-engine flying boat enroute from Rio de Janeiro to Montevideo and Buenos Aires on October 31, 1945. The propeller of the No. 3 (left hand inboard) engine separated. Debris struck the No. 2 engine and a propeller blade sliced through the fuselage killing two passengers The pilot carried out emergency procedures and ditched in a lagoon.[20]

Another happened on January 11, 1947. A Far East C-54 (the military version of DC-4) was enroute from Shanghai to Manila when the No. 2 engine caught fire. The crew ditched 81 miles west of Laoag in the Philippines. Seven of the 42 passengers and crew were killed.[21]

Stratocruisers, Constellations, and DC-7s were all victims of their engines and/or propellers going out of control. The first of these losses was a Stratocruiser flown by Pan Am. It was March 26, 1955, when the clipper United States ditched in the Pacific Ocean approximately 35 miles off the Oregon coast, at 11:12 A.M. The cause was the No. 3 engine and propeller tearing loose from the wing. All 23 occupants were evacuated, but four fatalities and one serious injury occurred.

Although the clipper touched down under near ideal sea conditions with little swell, contact with the water was severe. This dislodged life rafts from their storage bins and some seats were torn loose. The aft portion of the fuselage and empennage [tail section] broke off at impact, but the aircraft floated for 20 minutes before sinking. Approximately two hours after the aircraft ditched, the USS Bayfield, a Navy transport ship, arrived on the scene and rescued the survivors.

The fate of a DC-7 brought down by engine troubles is told at the end of this chapter while that of a Constellation is in the Ditching chapter. Aircraft, flight crews and passengers continued to be lost fairly regularly throughout the 1950s and 60s. This changed dramatically for the better when commercial jet airliners came on the scene.

Third Era—Enter the Jets

A quarter century ago, transatlantic air travel relied on a small number of "intercontinental gateway" airports. Almost all flights across the North Atlantic departed and arrived through these continental gateways, so flying from one continent to another generally required multiple flights.

In 1980, for example, traveling to Europe usually meant flying to New York, boarding a jumbo jet to cross the Atlantic, and then taking a third flight from London or Paris to one's final destination. Today, in contrast, people increasingly fly a direct route. Whether one is traveling from Cincinnati to Switzerland, Orlando to Germany, or Philadelphia to the United Kingdom, a single flight often gets us there.

These nonstop long distance flights became possible with the introduction of jet propelled airliners. Also, flying became much safer. Jet engines are much less complex and dangerous to operate over long distances. With the emergence of jet fighter and bomber aircraft in the early 1950s came the first commercial jets airliners.

The de Havilland Comet was the world's first commercial jet airliner to reach production. Its Comet 1, the first production aircraft, flew in January 1951. On May 2, 1952, the Comet G-ALYP took off on the world's first all-jet flight with fare-paying passengers, beginning scheduled service to Johannesburg, South Africa. It carried a crew of four and up to 109 passengers. For six years de Havilland was the premier jet airliner, but it was used mostly for flights over land.

BOAC's new Comet 4 initiated the first transatlantic flight from London to New York with a stopover at Gander for fuel on October 4, 1958. With a range of 2,400 miles the aircraft was capable of transatlantic flights, but not transpacific ones. BOAC's rival Pan Am inaugurated its transatlantic jet service three weeks later using the iconic Boeing 707.

The 707 used the same basic design specifications as the B-52 Boeing was building for the U.S. Air Force. The initial reaction to the 707 was not enthusiastic; its first orders were not received until a year after the prototype was unveiled. But with the support of a large order from Pan Am, Boeing took the lead in the market. Douglas countered with the DC-8 and the Convair Company entered the market with the 880/990 series built for Delta Airlines and TWA.

Air travel continued to grow rapidly in the 1960s and the transition to jets was complete by the middle of the decade. In the late 1960s, the new generation of "jumbo" airliners, led by the Boeing 747, incorporated major advances in every aspect of air travel, including capacity, range, comfort, operating efficiency, safety, and costs.

Keeping it Simple

The introduction of jet airliners, along with updated avionics, navigation, and communication systems, resulted in significant changes to the number and type of flight crew needed. Piston-engine airliners required at least a pilot, copilot, and flight engineer for short hops. For transoceanic flying a third pilot, navigator, second flight engineer, and a radio officer were part of the flight crew.

When jets came along a flight engineer was no longer needed to monitor the multiple systems attendant to each engine since the engines were far less complex. Reliable long range voice radio communications replaced Morse code which eliminated the radio operators with their wonderfully tuned ears and swift fingers. Navigators were among the last to go. These practitioners of celestial navigation were superseded by Inertial Navigation Systems and the implementation of a worldwide navigation satellite network (see the Navigation chapter for more info about these systems).

Now a pilot and copilot surrounded by a whole lot of technology are the only occupants left in the cockpit.

Summing It Up

The length of time from the Wright Brothers' beautiful hand-built flyer to the current mass of sleek aircraft has been only a few decades. Today, flying the oceans is no longer the adventure or the elegant pleasure it once was.

Although advances have made air travel safer, the possibility of ditching remains. Most of the ditchings have been due to engine malfunction while others were caused by running out of fuel, something no instrumentation can prevent or overcome. One was the result of too much bird meat for sophisticated engines to digest.

Whatever the reason, most engine failure induced ditchings have been deadly. Here's what happened to two aircraft that ditched within eight minutes of each other in the pre-dawn darkness on July 14, 1960. One made it down safely, but the other did not.

Pacific Night
Northwest Flight One
Philippine Islands

Right on schedule on the night of July 13, 1960, Northwest Orient Airlines Flight No. 1 lifted smoothly off the runway at Tokyo International Airport and pointed south toward Manila.[22]

As she had done dozens of times before, Yuriko Fuchigami, the pert Japanese stewardess, stood up in front of the passengers and recited her little speech about emergency procedures. The same routine is followed aboard every international airliner as it heads over water. Since the girls are cute, no one minds listening to the briefing, but neither does anyone take it very seriously.

Fortunately the odds are heavily against a plane's crashing at sea, and no one really expects his own flight to be an exception. Before the next dawn broke, however, the odds were to turn against Northwest's DC-7C.

The plane's commander that night was Captain David Rall, 53 years old and the father of eight children. Rall never got beyond the first year in college, but in 18 years of flying he had logged millions of miles in the air around the Orient, in the Aleutians and across the Pacific. His first officer was Travis Everett, proudly carrying his new captain's certificate for the first time. Theodore Wright, navigator, and Melvin P. English, flight engineer, completed the crew in the cockpit.

In the cabin were Edmund E. Zan, the purser; Antonio Suarez, the Filipino flight attendant, and Miss Fuchigami, stewardess.

At Naha, Okinawa, where the plane stopped for fuel, the weather briefing contained a warning to expect icing conditions about halfway to the Philippines. This was not unusual for the time of year, however, and two hours later, as the DC-7C purred along following the invisible sky lane known as Amber 2, the flight promised to be strictly routine. Altitude: 18,000 feet. Air speed: 300 m.p.h. Weather: clear, with a few cumulus buildups which were easily by-passed with the help of radar. Passengers: 51, including a tour party of 25 schoolteachers from the United States, two Army majors on their way to assignments with the United States Military Advisory Group in Saigon, plus some American and Filipino businessmen returning to their offices in Manila.

In the cockpit Everett and Rall could see each other dimly in the glowing lights of the instrument panel, while behind them Mel English made engine-performance recordings in his logbook. Outside, the stars swayed silently against the black sky.

Rall glanced at his wrist watch. It was 3:15 A.M. They were almost halfway to Manila. At that moment English noticed a change on the manifold pressure gauge for the No. 2 engine. The indicator had dropped slightly and, as he watched, it continued to settle, signifying a loss of power.

In view of the ice warning, there was nothing disturbing about this. It probably meant only that some ice had formed in the engine's carburetor, momentarily affecting its efficiency. Rall saw the drop at the same time. "There goes Number Two," he said casually. "Hit the alcohol will you, Mel?"

There is a switch for each engine that injects alcohol into the carburetor intake manifold to dissolve ice. This action should have solved the problem. A few seconds later Rall rechecked the gauge. It was still dropping.

"Mel, hit the alky [alcohol]," he said sharply, thinking that his original order hadn't been obeyed.

"Dave, I'm already on it," English said. "It doesn't take."

Quickly, secondary action was taken. The fuel mixture to the carburetor was enriched, the ignition was retarded and carburetor heat applied to the ailing engine.

The trained eyes of the engineer swept across the electronic engine analyzer, checking each of No. 2 engine's eighteen cylinders in turn. All patterns on the oscilloscope read normal. Oil pressure was up. Oil quantities correct. Just the same, English repeated the check.

This time the wriggling lines on the 'scope told another story. The No.2 engine showed an erratic pattern on the glowing cathode tube. What's more, the gauges showed that its oil temperature was rising—fast.

"We've got an irregular pattern on Number Two, Dave," he reported. "Better feather it."

"O.K.," acknowledged the captain. "Let's feather." Stopping the engine and turning the blades of the propeller parallel to the line of flight would cut down the wind resistance and keep the engine from undergoing any more damage. Flying the DC-7C on three engines would be no problem.

The red FEATHER button overhead was punched and the crew waited for the r.p.m. gauge to show that the engine had stopped turning. It didn't. Instead, the needle showed that it had begun to spin faster and faster.

Rall heard its distinctive, chilling whine over the smooth roar of the other engines. The FEATHER button was hit again and then again. Still nothing. The power setting for the normal cruise power was 1,950 r.p.m.'s. This was increased to 2,350, but the runaway No. 2 went ahead of them, closer and closer to the 2,750 safe-operating limit. The oil quantity gauge suddenly nose-dived to zero and the r.p.m.'s went up to 2,900.

Without turning, Rall said, "Ted, give me a position." Then as the navigator computed the ship's precise place along Amber 2, the captain went on the air.

"Manila, Manila, this is Northwest Flight One. Request an intercept by air-sea rescue, please. We have an engine malfunction and a runaway prop. We are on a heading of two zero five, one eight zero miles northwest of Jomalig Island on Amber Two. Do you read me, Manila?"

His emergency call was acknowledged, and Rall asked permission to descend. He wanted to get down into the heavier air which might help slow the wind-milling, runaway prop.

Manila granted the request. "Roger, Northwest One. You are cleared to descend to seven thousand feet."

Rall glanced back over his shoulder to see the troublesome engine for himself. It was the inboard one on the left side of the ship. In the cold glare of the wing spotlight he could see the unnaturally flailing prop. The ship was making a rapid descent. He called for flaps and speed brakes. They cut his air speed to 130 knots.

As the plane settled, Rall eyed the cloud layers below. Once in them he knew that he'd hit severe turbulence and rain. These he didn't need. Besides, an escort plane would never find them in that deck of storm clouds. He elected to level off at 9,000 feet—just above the clouds and out of the slamming and banging turbulence that could add to his difficulties.

Now the captain got on the interphone and rang the cabin to call Eddie Zan forward, but the alert purser had already sensed trouble and was on his way up to the flight deck. He had heard the change in the steady drone of the props and recognized that something was wrong.

"How bad is it, Dave?" Eddie asked quietly as he stepped onto the flight deck.

"Well, so far our destination is still Manila, Eddie, but I've asked for an A. S. R. [Air Sea Rescue] in case we have to ditch; I think you ought to go through the practice procedure with the passengers. But, Eddie, try not to alarm people if you can help it. I'll make an announcement while you get ready." The purser slipped back to alert his cabin attendants.

Most of the passengers by now were awake. The rapid descent and the flurry of movement by the cabin crew sent a ripple of apprehension through the compartments. The lights came on and the familiar crackle of the public-address system foretold an announcement.

"Ladies and gentlemen, this is your captain. We're sorry to wake you, but as you've probably guessed, we have a cranky engine. I'm sorry that I haven't relayed any more information to you sooner, but we've been busy up front here alerting the appropriate ground stations. Our destination is still Manila at the present time, but we have requested and expect soon an interception by the air sea rescue people. I want to assure you that we are not expecting any further emergency hut we ought to have a practice ditching procedure."

There was a quick sob from one of the women. She buried her face in her hands. Her husband put his arm around her, but could only continue to stare and listen to Rall's even voice issuing instruction.

About 30 minutes had passed since the first sign of trouble, and all efforts to feather the engine had failed. Then the engineer sang out, "Number Two's on fire." The red warning light glowed its silent danger sign.

Thank God there're no kids aboard, Rall thought, as he reached up under the glare shield to the fire-extinguisher handle. He gave it a firm tug—and waited.

There are two pairs of Freon bottles inside each engine. Rall fired the first set, and they did their job. The fire warning light went out. But the captain had no illusions that his troubles were over. Whatever caused that first fire would start another.

Mel English looked at the engine through the left window and saw sparks start to shoot out. Rall grabbed the intercom phone. "Eddie—evacuate the hazard zone, quickly."

Zan and the other cabin attendants moved to get the sixteen passengers out of the forward first-class cabins nearest to the engines. There weren't enough seats back in the rear, so the men squatted in the aisles while the women took their places.

Mel turned away from the window. "Looks like Number Two is grinding up, Dave," he said.

Dave turned back to his navigator. "Ted, how about giving me a course from here to a position directly east of Manila? If we have to ditch, I want to be over water all of the way."

In the cabins the passengers had removed their shoes and eyeglasses, taken all pointed objects from their pockets and donned Mae West life vests. Now they waited nervously. Most sat with their eyes closed, heads limply back on the seat rests.

The engine should already have been grabbed to a stop by the sheer force of raw metal binding on metal. But it continued to spin. At

3:50 A. M. the cabin rocked under a series of loud thumping noises. The engine was beginning to tear itself apart. The navigator computed a new course and handed it up to Rall. He nodded and went on the air again.

"Manila, Manila, this is Northwest Flight One. We are departing Amber Two on a course of 225 magnetic to a point directly east of Manila. Do you read me? We request fire-fighting equipment meet us at touchdown. We just had one fire and may get more. Do you read me, Manila?"

Silence for a couple of seconds. Then the excited voice of the Filipino radio operator at the ground station. "Please repeat. Northwest One, please repeat."

The crew exchanged worried glances. This was no time for the ground to get buck fever. Patiently Rall repeated his message and even spelled out phonetically the positions. "Please advise air-sea rescue that we are changing our course," he added. "Do you understand?"

The radio operator hesitated, then said he did. Rall thought no more about him, for he had the immediate business of trying to stop the runaway engine. Without oil to cool it, tremendous heat was being generated. Something had to give.

The cabin bucked under the uneven force of the grinding, wrenching action. Then suddenly Mel yelled, "There goes the prop."

Like a huge, three-bladed knife, the propeller cart-wheeled through the air, slammed into the fuselage, then whirled off like a banshee into the night.

Zan heard the slamming noise and knew what had happened. He ran forward, fearing that the prop might have slashed into the flight deck and killed someone. As he raced through the forward compartments earlier emptied, he saw the jagged holes in the upper part of the ceiling. Wind whistled through the ruptures. He reached the door of the flight deck just as Rall was ringing him on the intercom again.

"Better pre-position the life rafts, Eddie. Assign the men to help you on launching. Put the swimmers with non-swimmers. Keep husbands with wives. Use the buddy system. Get on the emergency lights."

Each one of the cabin crew had his own ditching station. Methodically they went through the routine that all had done in practice so many times. The rafts were taken down and put by the emergency escape hatches. Passengers were assigned to each raft. All loose equipment was stowed in the galley and personal belongings were even carefully put in a locker for safekeeping. Suarez and Miss Fuchigami served up iced tea and water to the passengers. Then there was nothing left to do but wait.

"I then asked for swimmers and placed able-bodied men in positions to handle rafts," recalls Zan. "We assigned the passengers to the rafts in their area. We had positioned two rafts in the tourist compartment along the over-wing exits, another by the main cabin door and another by the window exit on the right hand side of the aft compartment. All rafts were secured with their lanyards. We then instructed the passengers as to their ditching position."

Losing the prop was a temporary relief, for the plane was free of the drag. But now Rall could see a glow back in the engine where the crankshaft had turned red-hot, As he watched, white sparks began to shoot out from the magnesium casing, then flames licked through.

"Number Two on fire," called the engineer.

"O.K., let's fight it," replied Rall coolly. The second and only remaining set of Freon bottles was fired into the burning engine. The fire warning light winked out and, for a split second, the crew thought they might have the blaze snuffed. They were wrong—and didn't need any indicators to tell them so.

Rall looked at the white fury on his wing for a moment, then turned to his navigator. "Ted, advise Manila we've got another fire. And, Ted, tell 'em we're going to ditch."

That was it. The decision was made. Until then, Rall's alternatives had been either to nurse the crippled plane back toward Manila for a forced landing there or to court almost certain death by attempting a night ditching at sea in a storm. Now he no longer had any choice.

Rall put his ship into an emergency descent from 9,000 feet toward the water. As the ship plunged down through the rain and the mists that tore past the wings, he knew there was going to be no break in the thick cloud cover. On top of everything else, he thought with resignation, this has to be a blind landing.

The moisture only added to the intensity of the magnesium fire, and he knew that it wouldn't be long before the flames ate down to the wing spar itself. Once that was weakened. there would be no more need to worry about the ditching—or anything else.

Rall didn't have to tell his flight crew what to do. Already each was stowing away loose gear around his station. Ted folded up his little loran navigating table, which blocked an emergency exit, while Mel English broke out the Gibson Girl emergency radio transmitter, that would go with him into a raft.

"What's the fire look like?" Everett asked Rall.

Dave turned around in his seat and peered through the blinding white glare that already bathed the flight deck with a ghostly light. He could see the bare metal of the gears completely revealed now. It was a terrifying sight.

"Travis," he said soberly, "it looks like the teeth of hell back there."

Rall's experience as a pilot told him that time was short, that he probably had only a few minutes more to live. He wasn't ready to die, he thought, but he accepted the truth: I will soon meet my Creator.

Aft, Eddie Zan saw that everything was ready. The rafts were down and secured with their lanyards to the exits. The passengers were securely strapped in the seats closest to the escape stations. Miss Fuchigami and Tony had passed out all the blankets and pillows to use for padding. There were no seats for the two young flight attendants, so they just wedged themselves down on the floor between a bulkhead and a row of seats.

Eddie took the last precaution of having each passenger turn on his life-vest flashlight They'll have enough to worry about when they get in the water without remembering it, he reasoned.

Then Zan saw the navigator and the engineer come banging back through the flight deck door. He knew that they would leave their flight stations only just before ditching. This had to be it.

A Filipino woman began to sob desperately. Tony Suarez slid out from his position and tried to comfort her. Eddie figured they'd better get ready

"I think we're about ready to sit down, folks," he said calmly. "Please brace yourselves for the impact. Please don't be frightened. We're going to be all right"

But he knew that, barring a miracle the seven crewmen and 51 passengers had only about 90 seconds to live.

Up forward Rall and Everett handled the ship as if they were making an almost routine landing. "Bring the engines in," Dave ordered. Then. "Flaps up to approach."

Explosions were almost continuous from the engine now. Pieces of white-hot metal flew off wildly. There was no need to carry out the emergency-flare procedure, Dave thought wryly.

"I'll stay on the gauges. Travis" he said. "You watch for the water."

Altitude indicated 600 feet—then 500 feet. Another violent explosion, the worst yet, caught the plane. The wing's gone, Dave thought. But it was "only" the oil tank and the tires on the retracted wheels blowing up from the tremendous heat

"We're at two hundred feet." Everett warned. "Get ready." Rall threw off his glasses and pressed his face against the window hoping for some glimpse of the water. All he could see was the hellish blinding white glare.

Then Everett yelled, "There's the water, Dave. Pull up—pull up!"

Rall yanked back on the yoke and brought the ship up into a stalling flare-out position. His hands shot forward against the instrument panel to brace himself for the impact. Then the plane hit and bounced. On final contact with the water, the aft end of the fuselage broke free at the rear of the pressure bulkhead and sank immediately. At the same time the right wing was torn free at the fuselage and its two engines were torn out and sank. The once beautiful DC-7C was no longer a sleek, modern airliner but a burning, broken hulk.

Eddie Zan picks up the story: "I think the ship bounced several times and finally slued to the left and came to a stop. All lights except the emergency lights went out and the cabin started to fill with smoke. Also burning gas seeped in along the right hand wall of the main cabin."

The force of the first impact hurled Rall against the glare shield. The second bounced him against the flight-deck window. He slumped down, half-conscious, his leg gashed open and bleeding. His head reeled.

He shrugged, and held his hands out in front and shook them. As he watched his wrists and fingers flap, Rall thought, I'm alive. Then his mind cleared. He realized water was pouring into the flight deck.

"Travis" he called. "You all right? Let's get the hell out of here."

The two men threw off their seat belts. Everett dived under the seat to get the life raft free, Rall bolted back to the passenger cabin. It was filled with smoke and ankle deep in water.

The instant the ship stopped moving, Eddie Zan had leaped to his feet and told the passengers to stand up and prepare to get out. The crash had doused all cabin lights, but the emergency lamps glowed. The main cabin door was shoved open and one of the big life rafts was pushed out. The passengers nearest it slid out into the sea.

Suddenly a woman screamed, "There's a fire."

Suarez turned and saw that flames from the magnesium fire, floating on the surface of the churning sea, were drifting back toward the escape hatches. There was no immediate danger near the rear emergency exits, so he moved his people out there. Over-wing escape exits were too close to the fuel tanks to use.

Eddie continues: "We were afraid to open the over wing exits because of the fire on both sides of the cabin. Passengers were directed to the main cabin door from the tourist and forward first-class compartments. At this time, I heard Captain Rall call from up near the cockpit that if we couldn't get out to come forward. I hollered that we were all getting out in the back. I then noticed that the fire had gone out on the right wing side of the cabin and I tried to get the raft that had been prepositioned there out, but it was jammed on the floor between the seat."

The cabin was now heavy with smoke and filling with water. Eddie opened the window exit on the left hand side where he had been sitting and got the other raft out on the wing and launched it. He then looked back into the forward first-class and the tourists compartments and determined that there were no passengers left in the compartments. The water was then about knee-high in the aisle and the ship was in a deep slanted attitude.

Rall shouted hack through the darkness, "Can everybody get out O.K. here? If you can't, follow me forward. The exit here is clear."

Eddie yelled back, "We're getting out okay back here, Dave."

Just then there was a shout from up front. "Help me, will you, Dave."

It was Everett. Rall plunged back and jerked open the flight-deck door to find his copilot down on the floor, desperately trying to get the life raft out. It was jammed under the seat. After pushing and pulling, the two men broke it loose, but by this time the water was chest high. They shoved the raft package out their escape hatch, and Everett followed, but Rall stayed behind. He wanted to make one last check of the cabin.

"You'd better hurry, Dave," Everett warned. "It's going down fast. Hurry."

Rall sloshed back through the plane on a final sweep. "Is anybody back here?" he called over and over. "Yell if you hear me." Silence. Smoke filled the cabin, dimming the faint battery lights, but the still-burning wing fire illuminated the cabin enough for him to see debris floating in the aisles. No one remained in the plane.

Rall waded back forward and squeezed out of the hatch to join Everett. They hung onto a radio antenna for a moment to survey the crash scene, then pushed the raft clear and swam after it.

The DC-7C's right wing had been shorn from the fuselage by the force of the crash landing, and Rall saw a number of survivors perched atop it. Others bobbed in the water waiting to be scooped up by the life rafts.

Miss Fuchigami swam around calling to those in the water nearby to stay together. Those separated she herded together like a mother duck. "Please follow me," she said politely as she waited for a raft to make its way to them.

Rall and Everett in their ten-man raft paddled around the downwind side of the wreck collecting survivors. Rall eyed the wing and didn't like the idea of passengers clinging to it. It was full of sharp, jagged points where tubes and spars had been ripped apart. These were dangerous, especially in the dark. He yelled over to the survivors on the wing.

"Get off the wing. Be careful as you get down. We can't come any closer with the raft. That wing will punch holes in rubber. You'll have to jump off and swim to us."

Reluctantly the high-and-dry crowd obeyed, and all were pulled into rafts.

Rall watched the plane. It had settled lower and lower in the water. He shouted for all rafts to get far away from the ship. Then, about seven minutes after the crash, the DC-7C nosed down, its tail lifted momentarily high in the air, and slipped silently beneath the waves, The fire which had thrown some light on the disaster scene was gone.

Three 20-man rafts and one ten-man raft had been successfully launched—more than enough to handle the 58 people aboard the ill-fated airliner. But in the driving rain and darkness Rall still wasn't positive that all the passengers were picked up. The wind increased, and the rafts were soon blown away from one another.

He had the men in his small raft paddle toward the three bigger ones, and they were drawing closer when Rall saw a single light low in the water nearby. He shouted through the night to the figure that they were coming. No answer. The light just rose and fell on the wind-lashed waves.

Then Rall saw why there had been no reply. An elderly woman floated face down in the water. The captain reached out to the body and turned it over. The woman's eyes were open. Blood flecked her ashen face. She was dead.

Rall turned to the others in his raft. There was almost no reaction. He realized then that his passengers were so deep in shock that even the discovery of the dead woman did not penetrate their dazed minds. Maybe it was better.

"There are already eleven people in this raft." he said quietly. "I can't jeopardize your safety by further overloading it. We've got to hurry and catch those other rafts. The rescue boats will soon he here. They'll recover the body. I think we should leave her." There were a few murmurs of assent. Rall nodded, and Everett and the other men with paddles set to work again.

It took nearly two hours to reach the other rafts. Sea anchors were let out and canopies spread to protect the weakened survivors from the storm. The four rafts were lashed together. Most of the passengers were seasick from the constant motion and could only slump helplessly in the bottom of the rafts.

A voice count among the rafts established that only one person was missing. She was accounted for by Rall's grim discovery.

From the survival compartments, buckets and sponges were broken out to help bail the rafts. Shark repellent and dye markers were tossed overboard.

There was no immediate danger now, but as dawn broke through the gray overcast and the squall lessened in its fury, the question that nagged most of the passengers was voiced.

"Where are the rescue planes? If they knew we were going to crash, why aren't they here? Will they ever find us?"

Rall and his crew assured the passengers that the delay was merely caused by the heavy storm in the area and now that daylight had come, rescue was only a short time away. They hoped it was true

The emergency radio had been lost when Mel English put it down to fight the fire that floated into the plane during the ditching. By the time he had swept the burning liquid out, the water had been too deep to find the transmitter, and he had abandoned it.

Still, Ted Wright's position reports were right on the button and indicated exactly where the ditching would be. The crash site was close enough to Manila that the air-sea rescue flights from the United States Navy and Air Force bases should have been overhead hours ago. Rall looked at the cold and wet figures lying limply around him. They were exhausted in all stages of shock. Many had suffered cuts and bruises, and several had more serious injuries. Rescue had to come soon. It had to.

He tried to reconstruct what had happened that might have caused the delay. His orderly mind recalled each position report and transmission. Then he remembered—that last time when the Manila radio operator sounded excited. He took the position correctly, but did he understand the change in course?

Rall repeated the message to himself:

"We are departing Amber Two on a new course to a point directly east of Manila. In his hurry to pass on the distress signal, the operator must have assumed that the plane was then turning toward the coast. Instead, Rall had continued on a southern heading to get him closest to the rescue stations at Manila. If this guess was correct, the search planes were far to the north, sweeping over empty seas.

Eddie Zan was in charge of one raft. "I believe the lower station on my raft was ruptured by the jagged wing in the launching. The lower station was ripped and a small leak was found in the floor. The survival pack was taken out of the center section of the raft and the gear distributed. We patched the leak and then began using the bailing bucket and the sponges to clear our raft. Again, we had no panic or hysteria. As daylight began to break, a rain squall came up. We put up our canopy and collected some rain water in the plastic bags. Most of our people in the raft were ill at various times."

The rafts continued to drift with the wind, pitiful little circles of bright orange on a gray, fog-shrouded ocean. Then, faintly in the distance, Rall heard the throb of small airplane engines. His crewmen in their respective rafts reacted immediately. Smoke bombs and flares were broken out.

"Light 'em up—fast," Rall shouted. He had caught a glimpse of it—a twin-engined SA-16 rescue plane—but he realized it was heading away from them. Some passengers sat up and shouted and waved, but Rall knew the plane was too far away. Its scanners had to see the flares and the smoke.

He silently prayed as he watched the plane drone on. Suddenly it wheeled over on a hard 45 degree angle and came bearing down toward the cluster of rafts. They were seen. Help was on its way.

It was a Coast Guard Grumman amphibian aircraft. Two minutes later it was overhead. Dye markers, smoke bombs and shark repellent tumbled out from the open hatch. The plane circled low, around and around. Rall knew its radio operator was busy calling in other planes. It wouldn't be long now.

Excitement gripped the passengers now, and some came out of their shock-induced stupors. Light chatter began as they waved and shouted up pointlessly to the young Coast Guardsman hanging out of the open doorway. The leader of the travel tour group proudly held up his briefcase he had somehow saved from the crash. In it were the passports and the tickets for his traveling schoolteachers.

Another woman suddenly realized that she had clutched her pocketbook with her even as she floated around in the water waiting to be picked up.

That was the beginning of the end. The seas were still too rough for the small plane to attempt a landing, but the skilled Coast Guard pilot set his plane down three miles away in the slight protection of the leeward side of Polillo island and taxied through the boiling waters to the survivors.

By 8:30 A.M. the plane was at the rafts and began taking survivors aboard. A bigger United States Navy PBM flying boat from Sangley Point Naval Air Station joined the rescue effort about an hour and a half later. Neither plane could take off in the rough waters, so both taxied back to the comparatively smooth waters of Polillo Island harbor, twelve miles away.

Before leaving the crash area, Rall asked the skipper of the Navy flying boat to sweep the debris-littered area. A few minutes later a lookout sighted the pitiful little orange life vest and the body of the one victim, Mrs. G. Vernon Kelley of Springfield, Ohio. She was taken aboard, and as Rall looked back at the empty sea., the plane's engines revved up for the run back to harbor. It had been five and one-half hours since the ditching.

A young Navy officer cheerily came back to the bay where the survivors sat.   "Congratulations, captain," he said to Dave. "You did a tremendous job."

Rall looked up, his face mirroring the tension and the responsibility he had carried for those long hours.

"Thanks, son," he said simply. "But I lost one. They didn't all make it."

The Navy man shook his head. "Sir," he said, "it's almost a miracle that anyone made it. You brought back fifty-six people, alive and well."

Rall closed his eyes. "You're right. son." he said. "It wasn't me. It was a miracle that did it."

UNPRECEDENTED COINCIDENCE[23]

Just eight minutes before the Northwest Airlines DC-7 ditched, a Philippine Air Lines DC-3 carrying 28 passengers and a crew of three on a flight from Manila to Zamboanga City ditched between the islands of Negros and Mindanao. The pilot had previously radioed that he could not estimate his position and his fuel was running low.

He ditched about 40 yards offshore and near the mouth of a river. There were no casualties.

Lessons Learned

The Civil Aeronautics Board Investigation Report[24] of the Northwest ditching concluded that the No. 2 engine lost power because of a failure in the two-speed impeller drive system. This failure was allowed to progress until complete internal disintegration of the engine's parts occurred. Attempts to feather the No. 2 propeller failed because of metal contamination within the propeller governor and the engine.

It was also noted that the illumination by a one-cell flashlight permanently attached to the life vests of survivors materially aided the occupants in the liferafts in locating survivors in the sea during hours of darkness. Although Northwest Airlines had life vests with one-cell flashlights aboard this flight, the Board noted that such flashlight-equipped life vests are not a standard requirement for overseas flight of U. S. air carriers.

4. Navigation

Where Are We?

Getting from here to there and knowing where you are along the way is fairly easy on land. It has become even easier with the advent of computer-generated directions and car-mounted global navigation satellite system units. Even in the old days, when we relied upon road maps and friendly gas station attendants for directions, it wasn't too difficult. Getting lost on land, except when crossing the desert or traversing high mountains, poses few risks today other than running out of gas or triggering family disputes. Getting lost in the air is another matter altogether.

Marine navigation, the forerunner of air navigation, is a science that dates back thousands of years. Early mariners relied on piloting in coastal waters and on celestial navigation for ocean voyages. In the early 20th century radio navigation systems were developed to augment these ancient skills. By the first decade of the 21st century satellite navigation systems superseded the use of both celestial and radio navigation.

Although developments in navigation technology over the last 100 years have taken most of the uncertainty out of knowing where you are, failures in the technology and in the practice of the science can happen. When they do, not knowing where you are can prove to be fatal.

Here is a short history of navigation, navigation techniques, and how mistakes can be deadly.

Piloting

Marine navigators use charts that represent a flat section of the earth's surface. Using the charted location of land-based structures such as church spires, water tanks, lighthouses, or prominent shoreline features, a mariner can determine a ship's location with ease in clear weather by taking a bearing on a charted structure. Trouble comes when fog, rain, or snow limits visibility.

Printed on all charts is a compass rose which is used to display the orientation of the cardinal directions—north, south, east, and west. It appears as two rings, one smaller and set inside the other. The outside ring denotes geographic (true) directions while the smaller inside ring denotes magnetic directions. The angular difference between true and magnetic north is called variation. While retaining the classic north, east, south, and west notations, the contemporary compass rose is also divided into 360 degrees going clockwise from 000 degrees to 359 degrees.

Celestial Navigation

Celestial navigation is a far more complex method of determining location. Like piloting, it is based on taking visual sightings, but the sightings are taken on the sun, the moon, a planet, or a star rather than on land-based structures.

Celestial navigation uses a sextant to measure the angle between a celestial body and the horizon. This angle is geometrically related to the distance between the celestial body's geographic position and the observer's position. Making this measurement is known as taking a sight.

The chronometer is a second essential instrument in celestial navigation. A chronometer is a time piece precise enough to be used as a portable time standard and is used to record the precise time each sight is taken. This level of accuracy is essential because the difference of four seconds can lead to a position fix error of one mile.

After performing computations using the angle and time measurements, a process referred to as sight reduction, the navigator draws lines of position (LOPs) on a chart from each celestial body's geographic position to where he assumes he was at the times the sights were taken. A good celestial fix is where three LOPs intersect and is accurate to within a three-mile radius.

One thing to keep in mind is that a fix shows where you were at that time—not where you are now.

Radio Navigation Systems

Over the last century, the development of radio navigation equipment and techniques took much of the guesswork out of navigating. Radio navigation used radio waves to determine position by radio direction finding (RDF) or hyperbolic navigation systems. Briefly, here's how these systems functioned.

The first system of radio navigation was RDF. By tuning in to a radio station and then using a directional antenna to find the direction to the broadcasting antenna, navigators could replace the stars and planets of celestial navigation with radio broadcasting sources. The result was a system that could be used in all weather and at any time of day. Two RDF bearings could be plotted on a map, and where they intersected was the aircraft's or ship's position.

An RDF unit consisted of rotatable loop antenna linked to a degree indicator. On pre-World War II aircraft, RDF antennas were mounted either above or below the fuselage. During and after World War II, the loop antennas were enclosed in an aerodynamic, teardrop-shaped fairing.

LORAN, DECCA, and OMEGA were all hyperbolic systems. They functioned by producing a series of hyperbolic (curved) LOPs through measuring the difference in times of reception (phase difference) of radio signals broadcast from a master transmitter and one or more synchronized secondary transmitters at fixed points.

Global Navigation Satellite System

Global navigation satellite system (GNSS) is the standard generic term for global positioning systems (GPS) that provide autonomous geo-spatial positioning with global coverage. GNSS allows small electronic receivers to determine their location to within a few feet.

GPS was the first satellite-based navigation system and remains by far the most capable. In fact, it's getting better all the time with the launch of additional satellites incorporating improved technology.

The only other one now in operation is Russia's GLONASS. Europe is behind schedule with GALILEO, which hasn't yet been fielded. China is even farther behind with COMPASS, but may beat the Europeans into operation.

Inertial Navigation Systems

The Inertial Navigation System (INS) was developed in the early 1950s and is a modern variation of dead reckoning. An INS computes its position based on motion sensors. Once the initial latitude and longitude is established the system receives impulses from motion detectors that measure the acceleration along three or more axes. These inputs enable it to continually and accurately calculate the current latitude and longitude.

Its advantages over traditional dead reckoning is that once the starting position is set, an INS does not require outside information and it is not affected by adverse weather conditions. The disadvantage is that it only provides the navigator with an assumed position, not a fix.

Navigation Short Course

To plot a course, simply draw a line on the chart from where you are to where you want to go. Then, using the compass rose, determine the heading you need to follow. This technique works for relatively short distances but becomes more complicated when plotting a long-distance course over the ocean.

Once the course is plotted, you then estimate the time it will take based on your estimated speed over the surface using a technique called Dead Reckoning (DR). This is the process of estimating present position by projecting course and speed from a known past position. It is also used to predict a future position by projecting course and speed from a known present position. The position determined by DR is only approximate because it does not allow for the effects of wind, current, helmsman error, or compass error.

Once underway, you can determine your position by taking a fix using compass bearings to known structures or prominent land masses on the chart. Celestial navigation comes into play when you're off shore. In both piloting and celestial navigation, three lines intersecting in a small triangle constitutes a good fix.

Air Navigation

While air and marine navigational techniques are the same, some of the tools used in marine navigation needed to be modified to make them suitable for navigating through the air, among them the chart and the sextant.

Aeronautical charts show radio beacons, airfields, and topological information such as the height of mountains.

The aircraft sextant incorporates an artificial horizon which enables the navigator to take sights through a dome window in the top of the fuselage. Some aircraft sextants also have mechanical averagers to make hundreds of measurements per sight to compensate for random accelerations in the artificial horizon's fluid.

In marine navigation, plotting the courses for a voyage is solely the navigator's responsibility. In air navigation, before the introduction of modern jetliners with advanced navigation systems, flight planning was a team effort. The team consisted of the navigator, flight engineer, and usually the first officer (copilot). Today, planning the flight is the first officer's responsibility.

Flight Planning

Whether flight planning is a team effort or the work of one person, the flight plan components are the same. The flight plan includes departure and arrival points (airports), estimated time en route, alternate airports in case of bad weather or an emergency, the pilot's name, and the number of people on board. Prior to departure the final plan is filed with the local civil aviation authority (the FAA in the US).

A major part of the planning involves calculating how much fuel will be needed for the flight. This calculation includes the weight of the fully loaded aircraft (fuel, crew, passengers, baggage, and cargo), cruising altitude, and expected weather en route.

Of all the variables taken into account when planning a flight, wind has the greatest effect and, until the past few decades, was the most difficult to determine over the course of the flight. Due to the earth's rotation, the prevailing winds between 30° and 60° latitude blow from west to east, which is why it takes longer to get from New York to San Francisco than from San Francisco to New York. The aircraft has a headwind westbound and a tailwind eastbound.

The wind can also push an aircraft sideways, an effect called drift. Airliners used to have downward-looking drift meters that allowed the degree of drift to be precisely calculated during the day when the ground or water below could be seen.

Before the introduction of pressurized cabins, pilots could fly low enough to drop a flare into the water through a little trapdoor in the wing. By carefully watching the flare to see if it stayed in line with the tail of the plane or moved to one side, the rate of drift could be determined.

Clouds, which indicate a low pressure weather system, can extend from the earth's surface up to 35,000 feet or more. They limit visibility and their moisture can freeze to an aircraft's wings. The ice adds weight to the aircraft which in turn adds to the aircraft's fuel consumption. As ice builds up, a wing's ability to generate lift is degraded. In addition to activating wing deicing and anti-icing systems, pilots also changed altitudes to avoid freezing layers.

All of these variables are considered when calculating the Point of No Return, a term we've all heard. For an aircrew it is perhaps the most significant element of transoceanic flight planning. If something goes wrong after this point is reached, there is no option to turn around.

Summing It Up

Navigation requires practice to master. Over the years the vast majority of navigators have been skilled practitioners. Unfortunately a few have not. Even the best may be betrayed by circumstance, their own confidence, or a series of errors, which the was case for a Transocean Air Lines flight on August 15, 1949.

━━━

Compound Errors
Transocean Air Lines DC-4
Seven Miles Northwest of Lurga Point on the Irish Coast

A DC-4 operated by Transocean Air Lines ditched approximately seven miles northwest of Lurga Point on the Irish coast at 2:40 A.M., August 15, 1949. Of the 49 passengers and crew of nine, there were eight fatalities including one crew member.[25,26]

The flight departed from Rome, Italy, at 4:08 P.M., August 14. According to the instrument flight clearance filed with Rome Air Traffic Control, the planned route was to Marseille, France, at an altitude of 10,500 feet, then over Paris before setting course directly to Shannon, Ireland, at an altitude of 8,500 feet. Orly, the principal commercial airport at Paris, France, was designated as the flight's alternate if Shannon was closed due to bad weather. Clear weather and light to moderate winds over the proposed route were predicted.

The crew consisted of Captain Edward C. Bessey, First Officer Richard Hall, Flight Navigator James A. Baumann, Second Officer John W. Moore, Flight Radio Officer Robert D. Thomas, Flight Radio Officer Herbert Ashbell, Flight Purser Ralph H. Fisher, and Flight Stewardess Luigina Cerabona. The ninth member of the crew, Ruth Nichols, had no assigned duties, but was on the last leg of her attempt to be the first woman to fly completely around the globe.

Arriving at the airport 30 minutes later than originally planned, Captain Bessey divided pre-flight duties among the crew to save time. He, Flight Navigator Baumann, and Second Officer Moore obtained weather data from the local weather office. Moore then prepared the flight clearance which was filed with Rome Air Traffic Control.

First Officer Hall made out the weight and balance manifest, Captain Bessey boarded the aircraft, and Navigator Baumann computed his flight plan based on the route to Shannon via airways over Marseille and Paris.

Second Officer Moore indicated on the flight clearance that the aircraft carried 16 hours of fuel, while Navigator Baumann based his flight plan on 12 hours of fuel. After Moore and Baumann reported to the aircraft they discovered that only 11 hours, or 2,200 gallons, of gasoline were on board. This amount at a consumption rate of 200 gallons per hour, a standard estimate of the company, was not sufficient for the required fuel reserve of two hours normal cruise time from Shannon to the alternate, Orly.

The 2,200 gallons were less than the legal minimum, but Captain Bessey decided, since the weather was good, he could cut the mileage by skipping the Marseilles-Paris leg and flying straight to Shannon. At the same time, he decided he could skim around the edges of the regulations by changing his alternate base from Paris to Dublin. With these concessions, there would be enough fuel, and the captain did not spend the time to top up the tanks. Even 12 hours of fuel instead of 11 would have made a vital difference.

The pre-flight formalities were not followed: the navigator and the first and second officers did not check with one another; neither the navigator nor the second officer knew the correct aircraft weight and fuel load until after they had boarded the aircraft; the captain did not examine any of the documents before he took off.

Takeoff from Rome was made by First Officer Hall as pilot with Captain Bessey serving as copilot. After leveling off at 8,500 feet, 2,000 feet below the planned cruising altitude to Marseille, Bessey retired to the crew's quarters, and the flight continued with Hall flying as pilot and Second Officer Moore as copilot.

The flight reported over Marseille at 6:20 P.M. and over Rennes, France, at 8:50 P.M. The French coast was observed below approximately 15 minutes later than expected based on Baumann's calculations. The navigator then obtained a three-star fix which placed the plane 53 miles northeast of Brest and 15 miles west of the flight's intended track.

While Baumann was engaged in either plotting the celestial fix or in other navigational duties, Captain Bessey returned to the flight deck. First Officer Hall had been attempting to secure radio bearings, and although radio reception was poor, he was able to obtain a satisfactory signal from Brest. He also observed a second coast line ahead.

Shortly after Hall obtained the bearing, Bessey asked the navigator if they were just south of the Cherbourg Peninsula, and if the Channel Islands were off to the right, to which Baumann answered in the affirmative.

Based on a celestial fix taken after passing the French coast, Baumann estimated arrival over Land's End, England, to be 10:33 P.M. and at Shannon to be 12:10 A.M. Later, passing over what he took to be Land's End, Baumann revised his estimated ground speed to 160 knots and recomputed the ETA over Shannon to be 11:45 P.M. During all of this time, the pilots maintained a course of 330°.

Bessey descended from 8,500 feet to 3,500 feet, leveling off just above a layer of broken clouds. Baumann put away his navigation equipment in preparation for the landing. His work, the long-range conduct of the navigation, was over, and the rest of the job was up to the pilot, who would bring the plane in on the radio range.

None of the flight crew was concerned about where they might be until 12:15 A.M., 30 minutes past the ETA at Shannon. At that point Bessey turned around in his seat to snap at Baumann, "Where is Shannon anyhow?" Unknown to the crew, the aircraft had flown beyond Shannon at 11:00 P.M. and was now over the North Atlantic.

Baumann first tried to get a quick LORAN fix, but coverage off Ireland was poor, and that method failed. The radio range was no help either. A faint radio signal could be heard, but where the aircraft was on the Shannon range was uncertain. Breaking out his sextant once more, he then took another three-star fix which at 12:45 A.M. showed they were 175 miles northwest of Shannon. On the basis of this fix,

Baumann recommended to Bessey that he take a course of 130 ° for return to Shannon

At approximately 12:50 A.M., the captain turned the aircraft to a southerly heading for a few minutes and then into the recommended course. Sixteen minutes later, the flight alerted Air-Sea Rescue facilities at Shannon, giving its position as 100 miles west of Shannon, flying inbound on a course of 130° with an estimated ground speed of 140 knots. The west course of the Shannon range was intercepted at 1:14 A.M., and Bessey turned to that heading. By this time there was only enough fuel for another 90 minutes' flying time.

Two TWA aircraft in the area were alerted to the emergency by Shannon Air Traffic Control. One, captained by Charles Adams, made contact with the flight and helped lead it toward Shannon.

Despite the help, time and luck ran out less than 15 minutes from Shannon. Starved of fuel, one by one the four engines went silent. After a swift downward glide, Bessey made a good water landing in the Atlantic Ocean just off Lurga Point, the aircraft coming to rest in one piece at 2:40 A.M.

Quickly, the crew and passengers removed and manned all but one of the life rafts.

Seven passengers who didn't speak English panicked: instead of waiting to board a life raft, they jumped into the water and drowned. In a twist of fate, Flight Radio Officer Herbert Ashbell safely exited the plane only to be struck in the head by a piece of the tail assembly and drown. As for the plane, she remained afloat for about 15 minutes before being claimed by the sea.

Captain Arby Arbuthnot, commanding the second TWA plane, reached the scene just as the aircraft hit the water. After asking his navigator to get a good fix of the ditching position, he immediately flew to Shannon Airport, since it was not light enough for the crew to see anything at sea level. He discharged his passengers at the airport, quickly refueled, and returned to the scene.

"We soon arrived back in the area and located the rafts," Arbuthnot later wrote. "They appeared to be overloaded and we decided to make an attempt to drop one of our life rafts hoping it would inflate and land near enough to be useful. I flew over them at about one hundred feet and, when everything looked just right, I signaled the two crew members who had the raft positioned at the rear door to kick it out. When the raft hit the water either it did not inflate or it split open. In any case, it sank like a rock.

"At this time, I noticed several fishing trawlers about five miles from the life rafts. Due to the rough seas, the trawlers could not see the rafts so we made a pass directly over them and dropped one of our landing flares. This enabled the fishing trawlers to home in and approach the rafts. After a great deal of maneuvering, the trawler Stalberg managed to rescue 50 of the 58 that had been aboard."

It was two hours from the time the aircraft ditched until the survivors were pulled to safety.

Lessons Learned

The Civil Aeronautics Board investigation concluded:

Though some question may be entertained as to times, locations, and other data pertaining to the flight, there can be little doubt that the flight met with disaster because of inadequate flight planning and haphazard performance of flight duties.

As a result, the aircraft was flown beyond its destination and fuel was exhausted before the return to Shannon could be completed.

The navigator, assisted by the first officer, used or attempted to use four types of navigation—RDF, LORAN, visual, and celestial—to determine the aircraft's positions throughout the flight. Had he double-checked his work, he would have realized the aircraft was significantly off course.

These experienced men were betrayed not by equipment, weather, or technology, but by their own failure to follow the rules that they had followed on previous flights.

Copyright © Boeing
Boeing 314

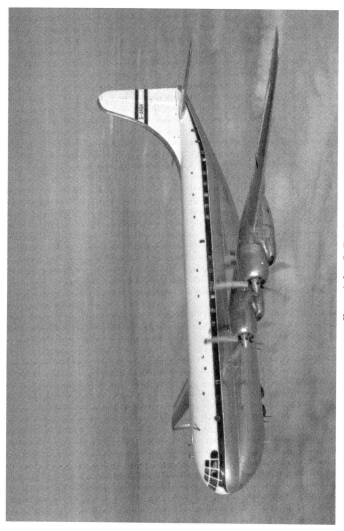

Copyright © Boeing
Boeing 377 Stratocruiser

DC-4 which was also the military designated C-54

Copyright © Boeing
Douglas DC-7C

5. Weather and Ocean Weather Stations

Mid-ocean Briar Patches

Accurate long range weather information is crucial for flight planning. However, over long distances the situation can change rapidly and not knowing what has changed may have fatal consequences.

Pilots and navigators in the early years when planning a transoceanic flight had to rely on weather reports sent by merchant ships to land-based meteorological stations. These reports contained information about surface winds, sea conditions, barometric pressure, and brief descriptions of cloud cover.

There was not a means of obtaining the velocity of winds aloft, temperatures within the clouds and of the large area a weather system covered, all of which was crucially important to aircraft. Also, since the merchant ships were only transiting a particular area there was not any way of gathering enough information from one particular location to accurately predict what the weather would be in 24 to 48 hours. This, in turn, limited the accuracy of long range weather predictions needed for future flights along the same route.

The ocean weather station concept originated in the early days of radio communications and transoceanic aviation. As early as 1921, the director of the French Meteorological Service proposed establishing a stationary weather observing ship in the North Atlantic to benefit merchant shipping and the anticipated inauguration of transatlantic air service. Up to then temporary stations had been set up for special purposes such as the US Navy NC-4 transatlantic flight in 1919 and Amelia Earhart's ill-fated Pacific flight in 1937.

As told later in the chapter, this lack of information sealed the fate of the Imperial Airways Empire S-23 four-engine flying boat Cavalier in January 1939.

The Beginning

Coast Guard officers Lieutenant D. E. McKay and Captain G. B. Gelly first became interested in oceangoing weather stations after a Pan American Airways survey plane, piloted by aviation pioneer Eddie Musick, went down in a tropical storm near Pago Pago while exploring a route from Hawaii to Australia in January 1938.

A series of experiments with weather balloons, some launched from Boston Harbor and others from cutters on International Ice Patrol in the North Atlantic, demonstrated the value of weather forecasts based on information gathered at sea. Captain Gelly, taking advantage of the Washington grapevine, leaked the test results to a friend who had the ear of President Franklin D. Roosevelt. The president, late in 1939, directed Admiral Russel R. Waesche, Commandant of the Coast Guard, to set up a weather observation service in the North Atlantic.[27]

WWII Atlantic Weather Patrols

In peacetime, merchant ships broadcast important local weather conditions to other ships and to shore stations. When World War II began in Europe on September 1, 1939, radio silence was imposed on all merchant ships. The reason for this was that any radio signal can be homed in on by hunting submarines, armed merchant raiders or warships. Thus, no weather reports at all were being received from the North Atlantic Ocean area.

At the same time the number of transatlantic commercial flights by BOAC and Pan Am was increasing. This activity required complete and accurate weather information, thus engendering the need for strategically placed ships which could provide the necessary meteorological data. The use of Coast Guard cutters to gather weather data was a logical result of the expansion of transoceanic air travel on the eve of World War II.

In January 1940, the Coast Guard in cooperation with the Weather Observation Service was authorized by President Franklin Roosevelt to use its 327-foot Secretary Class cutters to establish the Atlantic Weather Observation Service. The National Weather Service assigned meteorologists to each cutter since the cutters' crew were not trained in using the equipment or interpreting the results of the observations.

On February 10, 1940, the Coast Guard cutters *Bibb* and *Duane* assumed Weather Station 1 roughly 600 miles northeast of Bermuda and Station 2 located approximately 800 miles southwest of the Azores. The cutters were always on station when Pan American Airways (Pan Am) *American Clipper, Dixie Clipper* or *Yankee Clipper* passed to or from Bermuda and the Azores.

From the start there was a special relationship between Pan Am clippers and Coast Guard cutters. Lewis Tremblay, a Radioman on the USCGC *Ingham*, tells why. "Pan Am recruited a number of former Coast Guard radiomen because not only were they good operators, but they could repair the equipment if it broke during a flight. We were always running into fellows we knew or with whom we had mutual friends."

Cutters *Bibb, Duane, Spencer, Ingham*, and *Alexander Hamilton* conducted these patrols on a thirty-day out, thirty-day in rotation that wore down men and ships. Sometimes the cutters had to do back-to-back patrols with only a few hours in port for the crews to relax and break the tedium.

Bill Gallaher, from *Ingham*, recalls: "You'd go out off Bermuda or the Azores, but you didn't get to go ashore, and you wouldn't even see the islands. We'd just drift around and keep up about five knots, to keep underway and let the meteorologists put up their balloons and stuff like that. Very monotonous duty."

During 1940, Great Britain suffered horrific shipping losses from U-boats and the transportation by sea of new bomber aircraft became critical. Risks were taken to fly American bombers directly from newly constructed air bases in Newfoundland to England. This necessitated the establishment of a third ocean weather station about 500 miles northeast of Newfoundland to assist in the bombers' safe passage. The five cutters were now required to maintain three weather stations.

The escalating violence between the German U-boats and the British escorted convoys in the Battle of the Atlantic brought a cautionary message from the Coast Guard Commandant, Admiral Waesche, on July 22, 1941. He warned cutters on Weather Patrol to observe the Neutrality laws and regulations and to continue reporting all vessels sighted. However, now the reports were to be sent in code. The purpose for the change was help to safeguard the cutters and offer the enemy no excuse for any "untoward incident" such as taking a shot at the cutter.

As a result of the *Greer* Incident[28] on September 4, Admiral Waesche issued additional instructions to the cutters on Weather Patrol. These included special precautions against submarine and aircraft attack, notably by running dark at night, continuously operating the Q.C. system [an early version of sonar], steering a zig-zag course at a speed of ten knots from dawn until after dark except in heavy weather, stationing extra lookouts on each bridge wing and one astern, and painting the cutter's distinct white hull the Navy's wartime grey.

On November 1, 1941, by order of President Roosevelt the Coast Guard was placed under the operational control of the Navy and remained there until January 1, 1946.[29]

Expanding Coverage

By July 1942, fighter planes were also being flown across the Atlantic by way of a chain of U.S. airbases stretching from Labrador across to Greenland on to Iceland and finally England. Two more weather stations, one midway between Labrador and Greenland in Davis Strait and the other in Denmark Strait between southern Greenland and Iceland were established (stations "A" and "B"). This area was an area seething with the movements of merchant convoys and hunting German U-boats, a place always dangerous and often deadly for both the hunters and the hunted.

In September, the 250-foot Coast Guard-manned USS *Muskeget* fell victim to the German submarine U-755. Muskeget departed Boston on August 24, 1942 for her station 420 miles south of Greenland, arriving there seven days later. Her last signal was received on September 9, when she was waiting for USS Monomoy to arrive. Unknown until later was that Muskeget's signal was heard by U-755. At 3:16 PM Kapitänleutnant Walter Göing, U–755's commanding officer, fired a spread of three torpedoes, heard two hits, followed by sinking noises. No one knows if there were any survivors from the attack. It was four days before the USS *Monomoy* (WAG 275) arrived on station as Muskeget's relief.

A combined search by aircraft and ships was carried out on 16 September, but proved fruitless and the ship was reported missing. Muskeget's entire crew of nine officers, 107 enlisted men, one Public Health Service doctor and four civilian US Weather Service employees were lost.[30] She was the only weather ship lost during World War II although several others were attacked.

Just prior to the invasion of Normandy in June 1944, three additional ocean weather stations were located in blank areas far out in the Atlantic and the British Navy established one weather station about 50 miles west of the British Isles.[31]

On October 21, 1944, eight more weather stations were established. During 1944 the total number of flights across the North Atlantic waters was more than 20,000, or an average of 54 flights per day. The successful North Atlantic flights in 1944 depended primarily on accurate meteorological forecasting. Planes moved or stopped on the signal of the air base's weather officer. His decision was based on reports from the ocean weather station ships.

By the end of World War II in Europe on May 8, 1945, a total of 22 stations had been established between the Equator and the Arctic Circle.

World War II Pacific Weather Patrols

In 1943, the US Chief of Naval Operations, Admiral Ernest King, directed the Commander Pacific (COMPAC), Admiral Chester W. Nimitz, to establish two weather reporting stations, one north of the Hawaiian Islands and the other in the Gulf of Alaska.

As the Navy moved westward COMPAC established additional weather reporting and plane guard stations. The weather reporting stations were off routes normally flown by aircraft while plane guard vessels were on such routes. In general the plane guard vessels made the same reports as did the weather reporting vessels. On January 1, 1946, there were a total of 24 weather and plane guard stations.

Post War Weather Patrols

On March 15, 1946, the Navy turned operational control of the Atlantic Weather Patrol back to the Coast Guard, although it continued to keep directional control of the program. Because of personnel limitations the Coast Guard was experiencing, the number of U. S. manned stations was decreased at this time to six. The British also were suffering from the same limitations and from January through April they progressively withdrew their vessels until by May 1, 1946, the United States was the only nation manning Atlantic Station vessels.

In May, 1946, as the effect of the post war demobilization was fully felt by the Coast Guard, all but one station was temporarily abandoned. At this time Admiral Joseph F. Farley, the Coast Guard Commandant, stated that with the personnel and money allocated to the Coast Guard for fiscal year 1947, the Coast Guard would be able to operate only four Atlantic Stations. Early in August the Coast Guard was able to reestablish one station, making a total of two that were being operated, and on September 22 another station was reestablished. On July 1, 1946, the US Coast Guard received directional control of the entire program.

Although the numbers of military flights decreased significantly after the end of WWII the need for ocean station cutters remained strong since commercial flights had increased tremendously. The first steps to establish the weather patrol on a permanent peacetime basis were taken at the North Atlantic Route Conference of the Provisional International Civil Aviation Organization (PICAO) in Dublin in March, 1946. This conference recommended that a minimum of thirteen stations be established in the North Atlantic.

The Council of PICAO in Montreal approved these recommendations in the latter part of May 1946, and preliminary steps ware taken to implement this recommendation. Except for the US, the member nations of PICAO would not be able to contribute to the financing of the patrol at least for another year.

At this time, weather stations operated by the US Coast Guard were: C (Charlie), D (Dog), and J (Juliett) in the Atlantic Ocean; and N (November) in the Pacific Ocean.

European manned stations were: 4YA, 4YI, 4YJ, 4YK, and 4YM. The stations 4YA through 4YK were manned by British, French, and Dutch ships while two Norwegian ships covered 4YM. Like their US counterparts these ships gathered weather information and acted as rescue vessels for both aircraft and shipping vessels[32].

The busiest station was Juliett positioned on a major transatlantic shipping lane as well as on the favored route of the commercial aircraft flying from Europe to the Americas. Ocean Station 4YA was the quietest and coldest of the ocean stations.

Weather Patrol—Midocean Briar Patch

Typically a cutter on weather patrol spent three to five days going to and coming off of station and 21 days on station. A station (sometimes referred to as a Briar Patch) was a 110-mile grid of 10-mile squares, each with alphabetic designations (across—A, B, C, D, E, O, F, G, H, I, J and down—A, B, C, D, E, S, F, G, H, I, J. The center square was designated OS for "On Station")

A radio beacon automatically transmitted the ship's location. Overflying aircraft were required ro check in by voice radio with the cutter. The cutter then relayed the aircraft's position, course and speed as well as weather data. In addition, surface weather observations were transmitted every three hours, and winds aloft were obtained from instrumented balloon data every six hours.

Special Equipment[33]

The cutters were equipped with dual anemometers for measuring surface wind velocity, air search radar which tracked helium-filled balloons with metal reflectors attached for determining the winds aloft, and special thermometers to record the surface sea temperature. The air search radar also tracked any aircraft within range.

Types of Weather Observations

Observations were of three types: surface observations; winds aloft; and radio-sonde (RAOBS).

Surface observations were made four times each day. These included surface temperature, wind velocity, barometric pressure, and the height and direction of the waves and swells. This was useful in predicting local weather conditions for the next 24 to 36 hours.

The second type of observation, winds aloft, used a pilot balloon, filled with a specific weight of gas to give it a known rate of ascension. Initially these were tracked every minute. The observer took a sight with a marine theodolite, or sextant mounted on a tripod. From its relation to the horizon, known altitude, and its compass bearing the operator could determine the speed and direction of the wind at various levels. If the balloon went out of sight in a cloud, he knew the height of the ceiling.

The third type, radio-sonde (RAOBS) consisted of an oval-shaped balloon about eight feet high, usually sent aloft at night. Slung twenty feet below the balloon was a cardboard box containing a variety of instruments weighing about two pounds, the heaviest of which was a bank of batteries which provided the power for a one-tube radio transmitter. There was also an altimeter, a thermometer and a humidity gauge. A radio condenser composed of eighty-five plates with seventeen stops providing main contact points for a moving arm which moved across the stops in accordance with changes in air pressure was also included. Using RAOBS and radar tracking, balloon observers obtained data on air temperature, humidity, pressure, and wind direction and speed to elevations of 50,000 feet.

From these readings of temperature and humidity at various altitudes the meteorologist, when he had readings from four specific points, could make various deductions. He knew that warm moist air came from a southerly direction over water; cold dry air came from a northerly direction over land. With enough readings he could tell where the storms were and where they were heading.

Beating Boredom

No matter what their nationality, the crews manning ocean station vessels faced the roughest, most uncomfortable, and sometimes the most hazardous kind of duty. Added to these normal hazards, the European ships were often shadowed by Soviet ships during the Cold War.

The crews also shared the common problem of how to beat the boredom brought on by long days at sea, often under unpleasant circumstances.

For the men, recreation was limited to a game of volleyball on the aft deck if weather permitted, short-wave radio broadcasts, reading, watching movies on the Mess Deck or playing cards.

Sometimes the more creative crews came up with ingenious ways to combat boredom. The best way ever devised was by the cutter Matagorda on ocean station between Newfoundland and Scotland in 1951. Part of the cutter's job was to log the passage of trans-Atlantic airliners when they checked in by voice radio. After the required exchange of information, the stewardesses usually came on the air and chatted for a few moments. To the bored and lonely crewmen, the opportunity to talk with a beautiful woman, even if at a distance, proved irresistible.

The cutter's radar team dreamed up a beauty contest to select, by means of radio alone and sight unseen, a Miss Heavenly Body and a Miss Heavenly Voice from among the stewardesses passing far overhead. Luckily the idea appealed to the stewardesses, who became enthusiastic participants. Candidates for Miss Heavenly Body reported their physical dimensions, while Miss Heavenly Voice contestants read poetry. Since the radio could be tied into the ship's recreational loud-speakers, all hands were able hear the conversations and vote for favorites.

In all some 500 contestants vied for the titles. Reporter Bob Considine, a passenger on one of the competing aircraft, was fascinated by this unique contest. He featured it in his syndicated newspaper column which brought nationwide publicity to the Matagorda. After much soul searching, the cutter's crew chose Evelyn Conlon of Pan American World Airways as Miss Heavenly Body and Phylis Carrol of Trans World Airways as Miss Heavenly Voice.

Through the cooperation of their airlines, the women appeared on a network radio show. While America listened, the Matagorda's crew presented the winners with testimonial scrolls and engraved makeup compacts. Besides helping relieve the boredom of enforced isolation for the cutter's crew, the contest served to enlighten the public about the Coast Guard's ocean station vessels.[34]

End of an Era

By 1970, new jet aircraft equipped with inertial navigation systems relied less on fixed ocean stations for navigation information. Concurrently, specially designed satellites were beginning to provide weather data.

In 1974, the Coast Guard announced plans to terminate the US stations, and, in 1977, the last weather ship was replaced by a newly developed buoy. The European weather stations lasted another three years before they, too, were discontinued.

Summing It Up

Accurate weather information or the lack of it has always been important in commercial aviation and ocean weather stations played a significant role in the history of transoceanic aviation.

For more than 40 years Coast Guard cutters manned these isolated and sometimes dangerous pieces of ocean. They aided in the safe passage of countless aircraft and they assisted when something went wrong and planes where forced to ditch.

In most cases the planes were too far away for the cutters to help. Fortunately, three planes ditched within a mile of a cutter. One, Bermuda Sky Queen, you already know about and the second, Sovereign of the Skies, comes later. The third was a Military Air Transport Service (MATS) C-47 with a crew of four on board. That story is the last part of this chapter and shows what can happen without warning, and with unexpected pleasant results. However, almost a year before weather stations were established, the Cavalier, a British flying boat, was forced to ditch in the winter North Atlantic due to the lack of accurate weather information. Unfortunately for that ill-starred flight there weren't any ships near-by to succor it's human cargo. The following story shows how trying to muddle through a difficult situation proved fatal.

⋙⋘

"Muddling"
Imperial Airways Cavalier Short Brothers Empire S-23 [35]
North Atlantic Ocean

"The Cavalier itself lay peacefully not far from the scandal-smeared hull of the steamer, Vestris (1928), 300 miles from where the Morro Castle burned (1934). But it was no secret that the Cavalier, like these ill-fated steamships, had been caught in circumstances for which it was unprepared and had muddled through pretty sloppily."

From "Muddling," Time Magazine
Monday, February 6, 1939

The Imperial Airways Empire S-23 four-engine flying boat *Cavalier* enroute from New York to Bermuda, ditched in heavy seas 285 miles south-east of Port Washington, Long Island. Two of the eight passengers and one of the five crew members lost their lives.

Cavalier took off from Port Washington at 10:38 A.M. About two hours later the pilot, Captain Marmaduke R. Alderson, decided to climb through high cumulus clouds in search of better weather. Immediately after entering the clouds the radio operator experienced such severe static he was forced to abandon any attempt to keep in touch with land-based stations. Before doing so he sent a message to Port Washington saying "running into bad weather."

The aircraft had been in the clouds for 10 minutes before the engine power began to drop, but Captain Alderson continued heading south for 49 minutes before turning back towards Port Washington. He hoped to find another patch of clear sky and thus cruise in more favorable conditions. However, in making the turn, he had lost too much height to clear the low lying clouds and turned back to his original southerly course. But, the engines continued to lose power due to carburetter [sic] icing trouble.

Soon the two inboard engines shut down while the two outboard ones labored along at only partial power. Finally, one of those died completely. A four engine plane under good conditions can fly on two engines, but with the loss of the third one, *Cavalier*'s fate was sealed. Fifteen minutes before the ditching the radio officer sent out an SOS.

The sea was a roiling mass of towering waves and deep troughs making a safe landing impossible. Captain Alderson, with one sputtering engine, had little power to smooth out the landing—just one chance to do it right. *Cavalier* didn't get that chance. She struck heavily on the crest of a mountainous wave, snapping her hull in half. Fighting their way through the heaving, wreckage-strewn cabin, all the passengers and crew escaped safely. The Cavalier sank 15 minutes after she was torn apart.

There were 22 seat-type flotation cushions and six life preservers on board, but because the plane was so badly torn up, it was only possible to make use of eight of them, four of each type. There was, nevertheless, sufficient flotation gear for everyone.

Amazingly, only one passenger was injured in the ditching. He had been standing in the aisle when the plane struck the sea. Severely injured, he was supported by others until he died.

When she began to sink, *Cavalier*'s eight passengers and five crew members were left hanging onto six or seven buoyant seat packs. One male passenger was struck by wreckage as he left the ship, and drowned. A steward, holding onto other survivors, finally lost his hold and drowned.

After struggling for 10 hours, the remaining 10 survivors were rescued by the oil tanker *Esso Baytown*.

Lessons Learned

The formal British Air Ministry Board of Investigation reached several conclusions as to the cause of the ditching and made several far reaching recommendations. Among the most noteworthy was that passengers should be strapped in their seats at the take-off and landing.

No recommendation was made for achieving better weather information. The moisture-laden clouds and their freezing temperatures caused the carburetor icing, which in turn, caused the engines to shut down. Even descending into warmer air after that occurred wouldn't correct the problem. It was the lack of good information regarding the weather conditions, specifically cloud cover and winds aloft, that doomed *Cavalier*.

$\approx$

"Gee, it sounded just like Jimmy Stuart."
U. S. Air Force Military Air Transport Service C-47[36]
North Atlantic Ocean

The mid-watch (midnight—4:00 A.M.) on board the Coast Guard Cutter *Sebago* which was manning Weather Station DOG on the night of April 27, 1949, promised to be no different than any other night. Lieutenant Junior Grade (LTJG) Edward P. Sawyer relieved the

Officer of the Deck (OOD) at midnight and settled into another monotonous watch on weather station. In Combat Information Center (CIC), Quarter Master Chief Daniel L. Spillane was in charge of checking the planes in their flight over the ship.

MATS Flight 6396 checked in as Contact Number 28 at 1:13 A.M. ship's time. Routine information including wind aloft, surface weather, radar fix, and a special beacon had been provided with the receipt of her flight data. Fifteen minutes later the flight called in again and advised that they were having engine trouble. The pilot requested a continuous beacon as he was returning to the vicinity of the Sebago. The beacon was turned on, and preliminary alerts were sent out.

However, at 1:37 A.M. the aircraft informed the ship that: "Everything seems to be okay."

All hands on the cutter relaxed. Less than 30 minutes later their peace was rudely shattered with a sudden request by the aircraft to turn on all available lights as it was having trouble and might have to ditch. This time the distress watch was set throughout the ship.

The Commanding Officer of the *Sebago*, Commander E. A. Coffin, Jr., called all hands to standby to rescue survivors. Airfields and other weather stations were alerted and advised.

After it cleared the low clouds at 2:13 A.M. the aircraft was sighted circling the ship. Dropping flares, it continued circling lower.

On board *Sebago*, Boat Number 4 was lowered just above the water under the direction of Boatswains Mate Chief (BMC) Medio J. Schiavi. The boat was manned by BM1 Levy S. Barco, as coxswain. EN3 James W. Crawford was engineer, and Gerald W. Williamson had the bow hook, with Lieutenant Henry C. Keene, Jr., in charge.

The plane finally reached the end of a long, slow glide and plunged into the sea about a hundred yards off the portside of the Sebago at 2:51 A.M..

As soon as the plane hit the water, the boat was dropped the last few feet, it cleared the Sebago, and the first member of the crew of the plane was picked up from the water within three minutes.

The other three members of the plane's crew had remained in the plane. The boat approached the plane's cargo door and passed a line to the flyers who held the boat against the plane until they were all able to scramble into it.

Viewed by the men in the lifeboat the scene was both beautiful and dramatic. The white cutter lay hove to with all lights ablaze. Her huge searchlights turned the phosphorescent water into varying shades of green highlighted by a brilliant orange reflection from the flyer's exposure suits and rubber life raft. The multi-colored plane lay awash in the water with all her lights shining and her running lights continuing to blink on and off until she finally disappeared beneath the waves.

By 2:58 A.M. the rest of the men were removed from the plane and the boat returned to the ship where it was hoisted to the rail and the survivors and crew taken out.

Seven minutes later, the aircraft tilted further forward and then slowly slid beneath the waves. The crew, First Lieutenant Robert R. Bush, pilot; First Lieutenant John Jekel, copilot First Lieutenant George H. Behrens, navigator; and Staff Sergeant James B. Manion, radio operator, were all taken to the sick bay. None were found to have suffered any injuries except for Behrens, who had a slight cut on his forehead.

Henry Keene's Tale[37]

Henry Keene tells a more animated version of the ditching.

We were up on Station Dog. The Captain and I and two other officers played bridge until midnight, and then we all turned in. About two o'clock a young enlisted man came down and pounded on the bulkhead of my stateroom and says,

"Mr. Keene that plane's going to crash."

I said: "Very well."

He said again "Mr. Keene that plane's coming in to crash."

"Very well."

"Mr. Keene, the Captain wants you on the bridge right now."

Oh boy, I got up there. And this was an Army C-47 going from the Azores to Nova Scotia and it had auxiliary fuel tanks to make the trip and apparently he couldn't get fuel out of the tanks and it was running out of fuel so he came down on our station. It made a good landing: slammed in and the tail came up and nose went head down in the water. It was floating there with all its lights blinking on and off and everything was all right but again, the Captain says: "Take the boat."

So me and the crew in a power boat went over to the plane. The three pilots were standing in the hatch. One of them yells: "The radioman jumped in a raft and didn't have a line and he's down on the dark side."

So we went down and got the radioman back and I told the coxswain of the boat:

"Go right along the wing and slam into that plane, because I don't want to be set on that wing by the wind and current and we don't care how much we damage that plane. When we hit the plane, I threw a line up to one of the aviators and the three of them jumped over me, started jumping over my head into the boat.

The radioman yelled: "Hey, my B-4 bag is right behind the pilot's seat. Would you get it for me?"

And the last one says: "There's nothing on this plane we want" and over they came.

So we went back, hooked on and brought aboard the four survivors, no problem. The Captain and I were both pretty seasoned sailors at the time and we knew enough not to say anything to our command. The Command was in, I think, New York and we were under them. And we left station and proceeded at full speed for Argentia, Newfoundland. On the way, after about 12 hours we sent another message: "Unless otherwise directed, proceeding Argentia to offload survivors."

We went into Argentia Naval Base and tied up. We were actually operating under United Nations jurisdiction at the time and we had two United Nations observers onboard. When we landed and everything was settled one of them interviewed me with respect to going over and getting the survivors out of the plane.

And I told about how beautiful it was, nose down, tail up, all the lights going on and off, and how it gradually sunk but it was very beautiful even going down. That interview became a nationwide broadcast. Working at the Public Health Hospital at Staten Island a nurse named Jean Barr Macgathar was working on a ward. All of a sudden this broadcast came on the radio and she said: "Gee, it sounded just like Jimmy Stewart."

Well I think that that broadcast was the crowning blow and in two months, on June 18, 1949 Jean and I were married on Staten Island.

6. Ditching

"Kick, kick, paddle, paddle...."

Getting the plane down safely is only half the battle, the other half is surviving afterwards.

Knowing how to successfully ditch the aircraft is neither intuitive nor a drill that can be practiced using a real aircraft. Ditching techniques were developed over a period of time and at first they were done by trial and error. This also holds true for evacuation techniques.

The safe evacuation of the passengers and crew as well as insuring survival are dependent on several factors. Among these are water and air temperature, sea conditions, a person's physical condition and will to live, and in some cases the presence or absence of marine predators.

Generally, flight crews are well trained in emergency procedures, but even the best training doesn't insure that everyone will come through the ordeal alive. Even in the best of circumstances when no one panics and there aren't any injuries on impact, the pilot's success in making it down in one piece may be overshadowed by events beyond his control.

In some cases, adding to the physical dangers were the nerve wracking hours flying in a crippled aircraft waiting to ditch. Other times there were only a few minutes of notice before hitting the water.

In 13 of the 21 ditchings when the aircraft made it down successfully, everyone survived the impact, but not the ensuing events and circumstances.

Ditching Procedure Development

Pan American Airways (Pan Am) pilots were pioneers in developing ditching procedures for the simple reason that during the 1930s most Pan Am aircraft were flying boats. They were also among the very few pilots who were routinely flying over the open ocean. With the advent of World War II and the vast increase in aircraft making over-water flights, a more scientific approach was taken to developing standard ditching procedures. Because of its extensive use of amphibian aircraft in Search and Rescue (SAR), the US Coast Guard took the initiative in developing these procedures.

This development began in Greenland on April 9, 1940 when, by agreement with the Danish government, the US undertook the defense of Greenland. The Coast Guard's long association with the International Ice Patrol and the Bering Sea Patrol made the service uniquely qualified for Arctic operations. Consequently, during October 1941, Commander Edward H. "Iceberg" Smith, USCG was appointed overall commander for Greenland defense reporting to the Commander in Chief, Atlantic Fleet.

With the entry of the United States into the war on December 8, 1941, the need for anti-submarine and SAR air patrol in the Greenland area greatly increased. To fill this need Patrol Bombing Squadron Six (VP-6), manned entirely by Coast Guard personnel, was established. The unit's aircraft were the rugged twin engine Catalina PBY-5A amphibians.

Commander Donald B MacDiarmid, Coast Guard Aviator #59 and a flying boat expert, was selected to command VP-6. The squadron personnel included 30 officers and 145 enlisted men; 22 of the officers and eight of the enlisted men were pilots, most with considerable flying experience. All of the flight and ground crewmen had years of aviation service, every bit of which would be taxed to the limits during the more than two years of flying they would accomplish in the hostile North Atlantic. Hundreds of rescues were carried out by VP-6 during its 27 months of operations, frequently during high winds and near-zero visibility.[38]

Starting in early 1945, MacDiarmid, promoted to captain and now the commanding officer of the Coast Guard Air station San Diego, initiated a multi-year study of open sea landing procedures. Tests showed that landing and taking off parallel to the back side of a swell was the safest course. The results of this research work were published in an internationally accepted manual on air sea rescue techniques which is still in use by commercial airlines today.[39] This work focused exclusively on getting the aircraft down safely and did not include personnel evacuation.

Ditching Technique

Through the work of MacDiarmid and others it was determined that successfully ditching an aircraft is dependent on three primary factors: sea conditions and wind velocity, type of aircraft and the skill and technique of the pilot.

It can be extremely dangerous to land into the wind without taking into consideration sea conditions and the swell patterns. Simply put, a pilot should land parallel to the swells and into the wind.

For a pilot, the selection of a good ditching heading may well minimize damage and could save your life. It can be extremely dangerous to land into the wind without regard to sea conditions; the swell system, or systems, must be taken into consideration. Remember one axiom: *AVOID The* **Face of a Swell!**[40]

In daylight the easiest method of estimating the wind direction and speed is to look for long white streaks up and down the swells. Whitecaps fall forward with the wind, but are overrun by the waves thus producing the illusion that the water is sliding backward. Knowing this, and by observing the direction of the streaks, the wind direction is easily determined. The amount of streaking and density of white caps are also indications of wind speed.[41]

When on final approach the pilot should observe the surface of the sea. There may be shadows and whitecaps which are signs of large seas. Shadows and whitecaps close together indicate short and rough seas. Touchdown in these areas is to be avoided. A pilot should select and touchdown in any area (only about 500 feet is needed) where the shadows and whitecaps are not so numerous.

If the aircraft ditched near an ocean weather station vessel during daylight the cutter laid down a path of foam along the ditch heading. For night ditchings, the cutter deployed a string of floating lights.

Another key to a successful landing is to ensure the aircraft hits the water at a slightly nose-up angle to keep the engine cowlings clear. If not, the force of impact can tear the engines off and cause catastrophic damage to the wings or the aircraft. When jet aircraft with pod-mounted engines beneath (not inside) the wing were introduced in the 1950s beginning with Boeing's B-47 bomber, the pods were designed with "fuse pins" which allow the units to break away if necessary when an aircraft either crashed or ditched. This break-away feature was also used in landing gear. This prevents the engines and landing gear from puncturing internal fuel tanks, thus significantly decreasing the risk of fire or explosion.

A "Ditching Button," was first mentioned as part of Lockheed's four-engine Constellation in the 1940s. When the button is pressed, the aircraft operating system automatically closes all external openings in the wings and fusclage and immediately shuts down the cabin fans. The button itself has a guard over it to prevent accidental activation. The purpose of the system is to seal the aircraft to prevent water from undermining the buoyancy in the event that the airframe remains intact after impacting the water.

Once impact has been made, there isn't anything the pilots can do to control the aircraft and the tasks now focus on safe evacuation and survival.[42]

Safety Briefing

Since the 1930s when commercial passenger aviation started to become popular, airlines have included Safety Briefings prior to take-off. To insure consistency in information contained in this briefing, the FAA mandates what information must be read to passengers before each flight. This briefing must be given before takeoff if the flight proceeds directly over water. Although the wording may vary slightly, the basic information includes: number and location of exits, location and use of life vests, and location and use of life rafts and/or slides.[43]

On July 23, 2003, the FAA published Advisory Circular (AC No.121.24C) titled "BRIEFING AND BRIEFING CARDS" part of which included:

> An alert, knowledgeable person has a much better chance of surviving any life- or injury-threatening situation that could occur during passenger-carrying operations in civil aviation. Therefore, the Federal Aviation Administration (FAA) requires a passenger information system for U.S. air carriers and commercial operators that includes both oral briefings and briefing cards. Every airline passenger should be motivated to focus on the safety information in the passenger briefing; however, motivating people, even when their own personal safety is involved, is not easy. One way to increase passenger motivation is to make the safety information briefings and cards as interesting and attractive as possible.

This AC encourages individual operators to be innovative in their approach in imparting such information. Flight attendants will occasionally enliven this all too familiar information by adding an attention-getter at the end. My personal favorite is: "Once you have safely exited the aircraft, kick, kick, paddle, paddle until you reach shore."

Which brings us to exceptionally important factors in surviving a ditching—life vests, life rafts, and flight crew training.

Life Vests and Life Rafts

Aircraft life vest design hasn't changed since World War II, however, in our politically correct society it is no longer referred to as a "Mae West," but rather a Personal Flotation Device (PFD). Prior to the Flying Tiger Airline ditching in 1962, life vest inflation pull tabs were mounted by the shoulder and behind the inflation bladder. After that ditching, the vests were redesigned with the pull tabs mounted at the bottom and clearly marked. There are also tubes at the top of the vest for manual inflation should the automatic system fail. Each vest is equipped with a whistle and a water-activated light..

Detachable life raft evacuation slides were introduced in the 1970s on some commercial aircraft. Until that time life rafts were stored either in overhead bins, in compartments near the main exit doors or in the wings. Many smaller commercial aircraft in use today still store the life rafts on board in compartments near the exits. The rafts are equipped with an Emergency Locator Transmitter (ELT) radio, first aid kit, raft repair kit, sea dye marker, signal mirror, food rations, and water rations or a desalination unit.

The life vests, the seat cushions that double as flotation devices, and life rafts are all anyone has to keep them afloat for an indefinite period of time. No provision has been made or equipment included to combat the effects of hypothermia

Initially not all countries' civil aviation authorities mandated that life rafts and/or vests be carried. This proved a tragic oversight when, on June 19, 1954, a Swissair Convair CV-240 aircraft ran out of fuel over the English Channel near Folkestone, England and was forced to ditch. All five passengers and four crew members survived and made it safely out of the sinking plane. However, three of the nine people couldn't swim and drowned because there wasn't any life-saving equipment on board.

Crew Training

Most people understand it takes a lot of training and experience to be a commercial pilot. What many of us don't realize is that being a flight attendant also requires more skills and knowledge than simply being able to cater to the passengers. As in all areas of aviation, the process of identifying what skills were needed and then implementing the requisite training evolved over time. In the case of ditching training it was the growth of transoceanic passenger service in 1940s that caused airlines to began ditching procedure training for their respective flight crews.

At first TWA did not feel water ditching training was important, implying that it was more for theatrics than for having any value. In October 1947 those attitudes changed. On a flight between Shannon, Ireland and Gander, Newfoundland, a TWA plane began to lose power. The cabin crew were told they had seven minutes to prepare the cabin for a ditching. Everyone had to put on their life jackets and prepare for the ditching. At the last minute, the pilots were able to regain power and everything was alright. After that incident, TWA instituted actual water-ditching training in conjunction with the United States Coast Guard at Long Island, New York. Hostesses and pursers were taken up in a seaplane to simulate an actual ditching.

Transocean Air Lines went a step further. TAL's training division built a flight simulator for its cockpit crews which could duplicate flight emergencies including ditching. For the wet ditching drill, an aircraft fuselage was floated on barrels in a lagoon off the Coast Guard Air Station near San Francisco Airport. There the flight crews practiced getting out of the aircraft, inflating the raft, and safety procedures while in the raft.

This level of training continues today and has become even more comprehensive. Pilots from some airlines still train for ditching using flight simulators. For example, US Airways provides ditching training during initial ground school. During the training, the Quick Reference Handbook (QRH) Ditching checklist is used; this assumes at least one engine is running.[44]

US Airways' ditching training is similar to industry guidance on ditching, which focuses primarily on a high-altitude ditching for which sufficient time and altitude exists for the flight crew to prepare the airplane and its occupants. Furthermore, during ditching training, power is available from at least one engine. The training also addresses atmospheric conditions, sea states, and recommended direction of landing, based on the direction of wind and water swells.

The training did not highlight the visual illusions that can be associated with landing on water, as noted by Captain Sullenberger during post-accident interviews. He stated that landing on water was more difficult than landing on a runway due to "a much more uniform visual field, less contrast, and fewer landmarks." Specifically, when ditching or making a forced landing on water, a pilot is susceptible to the height perception illusion where the pilot perceives he is at a greater height above the terrain than actually exists because of a lack of contrast or visual references.[45]

US Airways and Airbus manuals contain very little guidance for pilots on flying techniques to use during a ditching to achieve recommended airplane attitude and airspeed at touchdown, with and without engine power.

Flight attendant training is more realistic. Wendy Stafford, a former flight attendant and president and senior recruiter of Airline Inflight Resources, describes her experience:

> We learned about decompressions and other in-flight emergencies, security, HAZMAT [Hazardous Material] and CO-MAT [Company Material].
> We fought fires and learned commands to shout during emergencies. We even had a simulated emergency evacuation, complete with smoke, red lights indicating fire and a rocking, contorting fuselage that we had to exit within 90 seconds—by jumping into a slide that was three stories high! We were given a packaged life raft and were told to toss it (TOSS 100 pounds?!) into the water, pull the red handle to inflate it, and get in with our bulky life vests on! Rubber against rubber makes this an extremely difficult task. I never dreamed what a fiasco my entry into the life raft would be. But after much tugging and pulling on the part of my trusted classmates, I finally made it into the raft.
> We then had to set up a canopy on the raft and identify all the survival equipment. Our group got entirely too much water in the raft and had to bail it out. Our rendition of "99 Bottles of Beer on the Wall" was not a required part of this particular exercise—it certainly wasn't in the training manual, and effectively unhinged our instructor! But how else were we to cope with the stress of a water ditching? We joked a lot along

the way, but still managed to keep in mind the seriousness of our training.[46]

In addition to a well trained flight crew, a successful ditching depends on a lot of variables. Sometimes human physiology is the greatest cause of fatalities.

The Human Factor

If not fatally injured when the plane hits, aircraft occupants in a ditching face a number of challenges while awaiting rescue. Among these are the potential for hypothermia, drowning, stress-induced medical problems such as a heart attack, and avoiding sea predators.

Hypothermia

In 12 of the 13 successful ditchings with casualties, hypothermia was the primary cause of death.

Hypothermia can be fatal. It occurs when a person's core body temperature drops below 95 degrees Fahrenheit (35 degrees Celsius). This happens when the body doesn't produce enough heat under conditions of extreme cold. Shivering is the body's automatic defense against cold temperature—an attempt to warm itself.

A person with hypothermia usually isn't aware of his or her condition because the symptoms often begin gradually and because the confused thinking associated with hypothermia prevents self-awareness. Hypothermia can occur even in tropical waters.

An example of how little time it takes for hypothermia to kill happened on board Northwest Flight 2, April 2, 1956.

The flight departed from Seattle-Tacoma Airport (Sea-Tac) at just after 8:00 A.M. Its intended itinerary would have taken the aircraft to Portland, Oregon, Chicago, and New York City. The takeoff was uneventful until First Officer Gene Paul Johnson retracted the wing flaps at which point the aircraft suddenly began to buffet violently and roll to the left. Captain Robert Reeve Heard believed that an asymmetric wing flap condition had developed and made numerous attempts to control the aircraft, but to no avail.

The captain brought the aircraft down smoothly. Although it took on water quickly, the passenger cabin remained in one piece and all of those on board were able to depart safely, most using their seat cushions as makeshift flotation devices. The captain and first officer, after taking a passenger count to ensure that no one was left on board, exited the aircraft through cockpit windows and swam to the left and right wings, respectively.

The Air Force Grumman landed near the ditching site within 10 minutes and launched a number of inflatable liferafts, but not all passengers and crew were able to reach them. Many of the passengers and crew remained in the freezing waters of Puget Sound hanging onto their seat cushions until they were rescued less than 30 minutes later by the Coast Guard cutter. Although they had adequate flotation equipment, there was no way to keep warm. The bodies of four passengers, including a six-year-old boy and his mother, and one male flight attendant were not recovered.

Over the years a number of studies have been conducted to determine how long a person can survive in varying water and air temperatures before death occurs. While these studies are of some use, the reality is often completely different. During World War II many men survived for several hours in the winter North Atlantic after their ship was torpedoed, which according to research, is impossible. They lived while others around them didn't. The same is true for passengers and crew of aircraft ditchings.

Drowning

Even in the best of ditching circumstances there's a possibility of drowning. While this might be something you'd expect to happen in an ocean ditching the following short story demonstrates that drowning can happen in knee deep water.

On January 16, 2002 a Garuda Indonesia Airways Boeing 737-300 ditched in the Bengawan Solo River near Yogyakarta-Adisutjipto Airport, Java, Indonesia.

Garuda Indonesia Airways Flight 421, carrying a crew of six plus 54 passengers, departed Mataram, Indonesia around 3:00 P.M and climbed to a cruising altitude of 31,000 feet. During the initial descent into Yogyakarta-Adisutjipto Airport the crew decided to deviate from the flight plan because of thunderstorms along their route. At 4:19 P.M. the flight encountered severe turbulence and thunderstorm activity including extremely heavy rain and hail.

They attempted to fly between two storm cells. As the airplane descended through 8,000 feet, about 90 seconds after entering the thunderstorm, both engines flamed out. The pilot, Abdul Rozak, tried to reactivate the engines several times, but could not. The plane kept going down.

As the airplane descended below an overcast cloud layer, Rozak observed the Bengawan Solo River and decided to attempt to ditch the airplane into the river. With flaps and landing gear lowered, he put the crippled aircraft down in a three foot deep part of the river.

At least 32 passengers were injured either when the plane ditched or during the evacuation. Santi Angraini, a woman flight attendant, drowned in less than three feet of water. The reason for her drowning in the midst of the evacuation was never determined.

Stress-induced Medical Problems

Heart attacks and seizures have occurred among ditching survivors. However, of all the ditchings the following is the only documented case of a stress-induced fatality. It happened on August 7, 1980, when a Tarom Romanian Airlines Soviet-built Tupolev 154B-1 twin-engine jet, on a flight from Bucharest, Romania, to Nouadhibou, Mauritania, ditched 300 yards short of the runway at Nouadhibou Airport.

Because of low clouds and haze, the crew couldn't see the runway until they were only 100 feet off the ground. The pilot immediately initiated the Missed Approach Procedure, but when the pilot felt contact with what he thought was ground it was actually water.

All 152 passengers and 16 crew members survived the impact, but a passenger suffered a heart attack and died before he could be rescued. An interesting quirk of fate is that the death toll would probably been higher had not the vibrations of an engine, which continued to function for a few hours after the crash, kept the sharks away. This allowed many of the passengers to swim safely ashore.

[Author's Note: Although this event this is listed as a ditching in Wikipedia, technically it's a missed approach.]

Sea Predators

Ditching in warm, open waters is more pleasant and more survivable than in colder climes, but it carries the added risk of shark attack. In three ditchings sharks arrived before the rescuers. One was the Tarom Romanian Airlines mentioned above, another occurred in the Atlantic Ocean, and the third in the Pacific Ocean. Here's what happened in the these last two instances.

A WESTAIR Curtiss-Wright C-46 twin-engine aircraft ditched at sea 300 miles east of Melbourne, Florida, at 11:03 P.M., June 5, 1950. The aircraft had 62 passengers and three crew members on board. Twenty-eight of the passengers lost their lives as the result of this ditching.

Initially 35 passengers in addition to the three crew members made it out of the aircraft before it sank. Thirty-four of them endured a night in two open rafts until the following morning when a Coast Guard aircraft located them. Shortly afterwards the USS *Saufley*, a U S Navy destroyer, drew alongside and rescued those in the two life rafts.

One survivor, who had clung to an uninflated raft during the night, was located, but was killed by sharks before he could be taken from the water.

In the third of these ditchings, although the aircraft wasn't carrying passengers it's a story of endurance with little hope of salvation.

It also marked the longest time period between when the aircraft went down and when the survivors were rescued.

At 6:41 A.M. September 24, 1955, a Flying Tiger Line Douglas C-42 on a Military Contract Cargo Flight from Honolulu to Wake Island, ditched in the Pacific Ocean, approximately 1,000 miles west of Honolulu after a loss of power in three engines.

On impact, the cargo broke loose and came forward, trapping First Officer Gin and Copilot Hightower, who was sitting in the radio operator's seat. Navigator Olsen opened the astrodome while Captain Machado assisted the two trapped crew members from their seats. The four men left the aircraft through the astrodome. Navigator Ventresa had been in the cargo compartment unsuccessfully attempting to jettison the bulky cargo. Before the cabin door could be opened by the crew members who were on top of the fuselage, the aircraft sank.

Three of the remaining crew members had life jackets on, but Captain Machado could not locate his jacket. Machado stated that he had no life jacket until after First Officer Gin and Navigator Olsen died in the water during the more than 30 hours awaiting rescue. Both survivors (Machado and Hightower), in addition to receiving injuries on impact, were bitten repeatedly by sharks during their many hours in the water.

Summing it Up

Successfully ditching an aircraft is a combination of training, preparation, skill, and luck. Surviving the aftermath depends upon many variables, among them coming through the initial ditching unscathed, having good equipment, not panicking, having favorable weather and sea conditions, and the amount of time you're in the water before being rescued.

In addition to the Swiss Air, Garuda Indonesia Airways, and other ditchings mentioned above, the following stories illustrate the best and worst case scenarios.

One was an ideal circumstance as well as being the first passenger jet to successfully ditch in a river, 43 years before the US Airways jet went into the Hudson River. The second happened in the North Atlantic. The third occurred less than a month later near Sitka, Alaska.

The last two stories are similar in that both were civilian aircraft chartered to the Military Air Transport Service (MATS), most of the passengers were military personnel, passengers and crew had roughly the same amount of preparation time before ditching, life vests and rafts were the same design, and air crews were well trained. The outcomes however, were vastly different.

This was due in part to the sea conditions, length of time before being rescued, and the pilot's choice of a ditching heading.

✈

Bridges, Spires, and a Tugboat[47],[48]
Aeroflot Tupolev-124
Neva River, Leningrad, USSR

The first successful jet airliner ditching took place more than 45 years before US Airways Flight 1529 ditched in the Hudson River in 2009.

On August 21, 1963, the people of USSR's second largest city were both intrigued and puzzled as they watched a small steam tugboat tow a passenger jet airliner along the Neva River. Passersby at first thought a movie studio was filming a scene, but then they noticed the plane's broken hull.

The Russian-made Tupolev-124 aircraft, then a new model, was flying from the Estonian capital of Tallinn to Moscow via Leningrad with 45 passengers and a crew of seven on board. The aircraft, built in 1962, was scheduled to fly to Moscow-Vnukovo under the command of 27-year-old Captain Victor Mostovoy. After takeoff, the nose gear undercarriage failed to retract when a bolt fell off the plane's chassis (the bolt was later found on the runway). During the flight, assistant pilots tried to hammer the trigger chassis and even cut the bottom of the plane from the inside to do so, but it didn't help. Ground control diverted the flight at low altitude to Leningrad's Pulkovo airport because of fog at Tallinn.

At 10:00 the aircraft started to circle the city at 1,650 feet, expending fuel to reduce the risk of fire in the event of a forced landing. The ground services at Pulkovo airport prepared a dirt runway for a forced landing.

Each loop in the airspace around the city took the aircraft approximately 15 minutes to complete. As the plane circled, the crew attempted to force the nose gear to lock into the fully extended position by pushing it with a pole taken from the cloak closet.

The eighth and last loop had begun at 12:10 when, 13 miles from the airport, the number 1 engine, starved of fuel, ceased to function. The remaining engine ceased shortly thereafter, with the aircraft above the city center, moving east over the spires of the Hermitage, Peter and Paul fortress, St. Isaac's Cathedral, and the Admiralty. Upon loss of power to both engines, the flight crew realized that the only hope was to ditch the craft in the 980-foot wide Neva River. With amazing audacity, the co-pilot joined the passengers and distracted them with conversation, while Captain Mostovoy turned the plane into a glide path above the river.

Eyewitnesses saw the airplane descend upstream along the river, passing the Liteyny Bridge at an altitude of less than 300 feet. They watched in amazement as the craft glided over the high steel structures of the Bolsheokhtinsky Bridge with approximately 100 feet of clearance, then missed the Alexander Nevsky Bridge by just 12 feet as horrified workers jumped from the scaffolding straight into the river.

The plane's tail touched the water, and the entire body glided onto the water's surface just 100 yards from the Finnish railroad bridge, narrowly missing both the bridge and the 1898-built steam tugboat *Petrel.* The plane didn't survive the ditching completely unscathed— the fuselage had been damaged and started to fill with water.

The *Petrel*'s crew thought that what they saw was a trick by Soviet scientists testing a new hydroplane, but Captain Yu Porshin was experienced enough to see the aircraft was in dire straits. Porshin ordered the barge that *Petrel* was towing to be unhooked, then maneuvered *Petrel* alongside the floating Tupolev, broke the plane's windshield, and tied the hawser to the plane's control wheel. With consummate skill Porshin towed the unwieldy aircraft to the river bank.

With the plane safely 'docked' alongside the river bank, the passengers calmly debarked through an access port on the roof. As the crew emerged, witnesses and passengers loudly applauded. A few minutes later, a bus picked up the travelers and their belongings and took them to the airport.

The heroic landing was hailed as a miracle in the press, and word of mouth propelled the story of the amazing rescue effort across the country. The authorities had no choice but to award Captain Mostovoy with the Order of the Red Star, though it was obvious to aviation professionals that his mistakes caused the incident. Captain Porshin was awarded with a certificate of merit and given a watch—a typical gift of that time to recognize courage and express the state's gratitude.

The plane was considered non-recoverable and cut into parts. The pilot cabin was sent to an aviation school as a cockpit mock-up, the chairs were sold to anyone wishing to buy them, and the rest was taken to a scrap metal shop.

Lessons Learned

The pilot's quick thinking and flying skills, ideal weather conditions, lack of panic on the part of the passengers, nearby rescue assistance, and a fair amount of luck contributed to making this a textbook case of what to do when ditching on a river. It is also the only ditching which, upon reflection, has any humor in it.

The Face of a Swell[49]
Flying Tiger Line Lockheed Constellation Flight 923
560 Nautical Miles West of Shannon, Ireland

On September 23, 1962, at 10:00 P.M. Greenwich Mean Time, a Flying Tiger Line Lockheed Super Constellation, under contract to MATS, ditched at sea approximately 560 nautical miles west of Shannon, Ireland. It carried 68 passengers and eight crewmembers. Of these, 24 passengers and four crewmembers died after the aircraft was in the water.

The passenger flight was from McGuire Air Force Base, New Jersey, to Frankfurt-Rhein Main Airport, Germany, with a scheduled refueling stop in Gander, Newfoundland. The original flight crew from McGuire was replaced by a new one in Gander. The members on the Gander to Frankfurt leg consisted of Captain John D. Murray, Copilot Robert W. Parker, Flight Engineer James E. Garrett, Jr., and Navigator Samuel P. Nicholson. Stewardesses Elizabeth A. Sims, Carol Ann Gould, Ruth Mudd, and Jacqueline L. Brotman were on board when the aircraft left McGuire and remained with it on the leg from Gander to Germany.

Carol Ann Gould was a last minute addition to the crew. She was staying with a friend when, at 4:30 A.M. the phone rang, jolting her awake. It was an unexpected call from the back office of Flying Tiger Airlines. Carol remembers the conversation.

"We need you to fill in for a stewardess who is sick. It will be double time," said the man from the back office of Flying Tiger Airlines.

"When I got to the airport the head stewardess, Betty Sims, was beaming. She greeted me warmly: 'We know you've been out all night and you're tired, you can sleep. We just need your body on board to meet regulations. We are heading over to McGuire Air base to pick up soldiers and take them to Germany.'"

The aircraft departed McGuire AFB at 11:45A.M, with 68 passengers, including Army paratroopers on their first overseas assign-

124 MICHAEL G. WALLING

ment, service members and their families. Among these was Captain Juan G. Figueroa, an Air Force doctor, and his wife, Carmen, who were going to Germany for a vacation.

Upon departure the stewardesses briefed the passengers on over-water emergency procedures. Between McGuire and Gander the navigator calculated his Equal Time Point (ETP) and the Point of No Return (PNR) for the Gander-Frankfurt leg and placed these on the appropriate navigational chart. These calculations were based upon the weather information and weather charts provided by U. S. Air Force personnel at McGuire AFB. The flight to Gander was routine. After the new flight crew took over and refueling was completed, the aircraft took off at 5:09 P.M. on the transatlantic leg of her journey.

At 7:20 P.M. the aircraft passed over the USCGC *Owasco* manning Ocean Station Charlie. John E. Ulibarri, a Radarman Second Class, was on duty and recalls:

"I remember working Flight 923 and talking with the pilot, Captain John D. Murray. After relaying Flying Tiger's position, speed, and additional information, Captain Murray wanted to know if I was interested in talking with the stewardess. Being at sea for weeks at a time, I jumped at the chance to converse with a female voice, a good distraction.

A stewardess came on the radio and we joked back and forth for a couple of minutes.

'Do you sailors ever get lonely in the middle of the ocean?' she inquired, to which I replied, 'Of course we do; there are no girls to talk to.' When she asked if talking to her helped, I told her that the only thing better would be to be in the airplane with her. She laughed and said, 'Maybe next time.'

"We signed off, and the flight continued east."

Approximately three hours after departing Gander a fire developed in the No. 3 engine. This engine was shut down and its propeller feathered. A few minutes later the propeller of No. 1 engine oversped when the flight engineer inadvertently closed the No. 1 engine firewall shutoff valve. This engine was also shut down and the propeller feathered. At this time the captain altered course to proceed to Shannon. After flying approximately one hour, the No. 2 engine developed trouble and the aircraft, with three bad engines, was in serious trouble.

At 8:25 P.M., the aircraft requested sea conditions from Gander Radio. These were later given by an eastbound DC-7 (identified by the call sign Riddle 18H) as winds from 260 degrees at 28 knots; primary swells from 260 degrees, 8 to 12 feet high; secondary swells from 300 degrees, eight feet high.

The requested escort aircraft, a U.S. Air Force C-118 four engine aircraft, piloted by Lieutenant Joseph K. Lewis, and Riddle 18H were in visual contact shortly before 9:00 P.M. About this time the No. 2 engine failed; however, its propeller was not feathered. Captain Murray turned on the public address system and said: "Ladies and gentlemen, this is the captain speaking. We are going to ditch."

After the second engine failure, the senior stewardess, Betty Simms, announced over the loudspeaker system that they would conduct a ditching drill, at the same time assuring the passengers that the aircraft could proceed to Shannon on two engines. She then called attention to a ditching folder inside the pocket behind each seat. The three remaining stewardesses circulated among the cabin passengers and assisted in explaining the ditching procedure.

All of the passengers donned lifejackets and were instructed not to inflate them until they were outside the aircraft. None of the lifejackets were equipped with lights.

Sometime before ditching, two soldier passengers, at the direction of the crew, removed the emergency liferaft stowed in the crew compartment and placed it in front of the left rear main exit door where it was tied down. The door between the crew compartment and the main cabin was removed and stowed in the left forward coat closet. The stewardesses requested the passengers to remove dentures, pens, pencils, glasses, and other sharp objects from their persons and to place them in the pockets of the seatbacks.

Passengers were asked if they had any knives or flashlights and those collected were then distributed to certain passengers who had been given special duties such as opening emergency exits and launching liferafts. According to the passengers, most of the stewardesses did not have knives or flashlights, as required. Passengers' shoes and boots were also collected and these were stowed in the forward lavatory.

Many paratroopers tried to act with bravado. One group filled plastic bags with sandwiches and told stewardess Carol Gould to join them on their raft.

Shortly before the ditching, Nicholson, the navigator, went into the cabin and removed the tie-down strap from the liferaft. He then seated himself in an aisle seat which was in the last row on the left side just forward of the main cabin door.

A ditching heading of 265 degrees magnetic was then decided upon and C-118 was alerted to stand by. Then Captain Murray turned to the left in order to obtain the heading of 265 degrees.

Just prior to impact Murray turned on the landing lights and cut the power on the No. 4 engine. The plan was to land just past the top of a swell. However, just before impact the nose of the aircraft was brought around parallel to the face of the approaching swell and ditching was accomplished into the swell. After initial impact, there were no skips or subsequent impacts.

The time was 11:12 P.M.

The impact threw some passengers forward when seats broke loose. Water poured in through the bottom of the plane. It was pitch black and little more than shadows could be seen.

Captain Murray's head struck the instrument panel. He later recalled that the copilot got out of his seat and asked him: "You all right John?" He answered, "Yes."

Murray got up and followed the copilot and the flight engineer out of the cockpit into the main cabin compartment. Upon reaching the cabin he remembered his flashlight and went back into the cockpit and retrieved it. Returning from the cockpit he said he observed the cabin to be clear of all persons. However, he noticed some seats piled up in the rear of the cabin on the right side, but blood in his eyes from a cut on his forehead prevented good vision.

Captain Murray then left the aircraft through the forward left emergency over-the-wing exit and inflated his lifejacket.

Nicholson had some difficulty in opening the main cabin door. Wing exits were opened easily with the exception of the aft over-the-wing exit on the right side, which was opened after moving a seat which had partially blocked this exit. Immediately after opening the main cabin door, Nicholson pushed out the liferaft, but forgot to tie the lanyard provided for the liferafts' retention to the aircraft and the raft drifted away. Jumping in after it, he managed to inflate it, although upside down with its emergency lights facing down.

One survivor stated that he stood on the right wing after evacuating the cabin, some recalled observing the right wing while exiting the aircraft, but other survivors stated they saw no right wing.

During the evacuation of the aircraft a few of the survivors said they could see clearly, and others said they could hardly see at all. However, by following other people they were able to find an exit. When the last passengers left the aircraft the water inside was at least waist deep. A passenger who indicated that he was the last one to leave said that he did not see anyone remaining in the aircraft, although, he added, it was possible that some of the broken seats may have concealed someone.

The aircraft sank five minutes after impact.

In addition to the 25-man liferaft stowed in the crew compartment, the aircraft carried four 25-man liferafts which were stowed in four compartments, two in each wing aft of the rear spar. A cable control, actuated by a handle located inside the jamb of the aft over-the-wing exits, sequentially unlatches the wing compartments' cover doors and opens the valves to the CO_2 cylinder of each raft on that side of the aircraft.

As each raft inflates it ejects itself automatically from the compartment. The stowed rafts in the left wing can also be released by actuating a lever in the cockpit. In addition to these releases there is a release mechanism on each wing's liferaft compartment.

None of the liferafts stowed in the wings were seen by the survivors during the evacuation; however, all rafts were later recovered. There was no evidence that these rafts were used by any of the people who didn't survive.

Meanwhile, Carol Gould quickly removed the emergency window and shouted for the passengers to follow her. She was anxious to drop down onto the left wing and open the raft compartment door. As she looked down, she saw there was no wing; it had sheared off on impact.

Twenty foot waves pitched the survivors violently in and under the frigid water. One huge wave swept Carol away from the plane while its undertow pulled Garrett directly into the jagged edge of the broken wing, killing him instantly.

The numbing cold and confusion left Carol in a coma-like state. The only clue she was alive was the sound of her own heartbeat. She fought the urge to give up and swam upward. As she broke through the debris-ridden surface Carol gulped for air and cried out "I will not die this way." She inflated only the left side of her inflatable life vest, thinking she might need the other side later.

The survivors alternately swam and treaded water until they eventually found the raft. Some said they saw a light, but it could not be established whether they saw the automatically activated lights on the raft or the flashlight carried by the captain. A total of 51 persons including Murray, Nicholson and Gould swam to the raft and boarded it. As this number exceeded the capacity of the raft by over 100 percent, the crowded conditions restricted movement.

Badly overloaded, the raft took on water over the sides. Bailing was almost continuous throughout the entire time on the raft and it was necessary for those on the raft to hold the heads of others out of the water.

Somehow the small grey raft remained intact. A few passengers had broken bones and internal injuries. Many had second degree burns aggravated by the constant chafing of their clothing as the waves buffeted them. Nearly all were suffering varying degrees of shock and exposure.

Suddenly, they heard propellers overhead as the C-118 swooped down and dropped a bright red flare. Carol Gould remembered its eerie glow. "When it first dropped it was like daytime on the raft. It was good, but it wasn't. I could see everyone around me and they were all bloody. The water in the raft was turning a sickening red.

"Private Brown was bleeding so badly from the big gash on his head that I knew something had to be done. Then, I remembered my slip. I took it off and made a compress out of it and put it on his head; then a wave washed it off. The only way to keep it there was to hold it. He blacked out a few times."

Aircraft were overhead continuously from the time of ditching. Among them were three Albatross amphibian search aircraft from Prestwick, Scotland. Originally their pilots had hoped to land alongside any rafts they spotted, but the heavy seas made this impossible. They were forced to head back to base for more fuel and to get ready for another try.

Roughly four hours later the small, 150-foot long Swiss freighter S. S. *Celerina* spotted the raft after being directed to the scene by the C118.

Celerina's sailors threw rope ladders over the side, but by now the seas had reached 20 feet. At times the survivors were level with the deck of the vessel, only to fall below the waterline the next moment.

From the raft, Murray grabbed onto one ladder but fell back into the sea. Paratrooper Fred Caruso grabbed him by the shirt and pulled him back into the raft. One by one the exhausted survivors pulled their way up the ladders into the arms of sailors.

Once on deck, a sailor gave Carol a shot of whiskey and it warmed her. She searched the deck for Doctor Figueroa and became his assistant, treating the wounded. Passengers remember that she seemed to be everywhere, giving comfort and medicine.

Carol paused only to look out to sea, hoping to glimpse another raft, hoping to find her co-stewardesses. Betty had been sitting just behind Carol on the plane. Her last words were to reassure Carol on how to retrieve the raft once on the wing. "You will do fine, Carol, just fine."

Throughout the next hour *Celerina*'s crew continued rescuing survivors. No one realized three people in the raft had died during the night: two servicemen and a woman. The last man to exit the life raft had been holding his wife's body; she had perished during the night, he had not known.

Later the sailors informed Carol that three empty rafts were picked up by other ships in the area. Seven bodies were recovered near the ditch site, those of Stewardess Brotman, Engineer Garrett, copilot Parker, and four servicemen. The other eighteen were never found.

As soon as he got aboard *Celerina*, Dr. Figueroa stripped off his clothing, put on an old, greasy pair of pants and a shirt donated by a member of the *Celerina*'s crew and went to work. He treated the injured, whose wounds ranged from severe burns to deep slashes as well as shock and exposure.

Asked in a interview how he kept going although himself a victim of the crash, he modestly replied: "I don't know. I guess it was a sense of duty that kept me going. It was something that had to be done."

The doctor said he was too busy to stop, even though he had difficulty seeing—his glasses were lost in the crash. "We worked with what we could find in the ship's emergency kit and a Canadian helicopter from the aircraft carrier HMCS *Bonaventure* brought some supplies, but that proved to be not enough. So then we had to have the air evacuation people take them off," he added.

Seventeen of the most severely hurt were airlifted by helicopter off the ship to the HMCS *Bonaventure*.

When the aircraft ditched, *Owasco*, then 10 hours away, departed Ocean Station Charlie and plowed through the night toward the crash site. Electricians Mate Third Class Phil Gorman remembers: "I stood watch in my slicks on the forward-most deck above the bridge in the rain and spray from the rough water, staring into the wind and rain for hours.

At 6:00 A.M., September 24, *Owasco* arrived on scene. Electricians Mate 3rd Class Phil Gorman recalls: "The port bow watch spotted a yellow raft. Out went a Monomoy life boat, which snagged a life raft. Nothing. The Mae West's were empty and that's all there was in the raft. It didn't make sense. It was morning before anyone was found. The first, the body of the stewardess who Ulibarri had been talking to was found floating face down. Then another body, a young Marine [sic]. That was all."

The bodies on board *Owasco* were later picked up by a helicopter from *Bonaventure* and taken to Scotland.

Stewardess Ruth Mudd was on her last flight as a crew member after receiving notice from the airline that she was being furloughed. Chief Stewardess Betty A. Sims, married secretly two weeks before, had given notice this was her last trip. Ruth Mudd's body was not recovered. Carol Ann Gould was the only stewardess to survive the ditching.

Lessons Learned

In each aircraft accident the Civil Aeronautics Board (CAB) reviews the factual data developed by its investigators to determine whether improvements are needed which would enhance the survivability of a similar accident. This accident was no exception and certain items are considered to fall in this category.

The CAB investigation determined the probable cause of this accident was the failure of two of the aircrafts four engines, and improper action of the flight engineer, which disabled a third engine, thereby necessitating a ditching at sea. The unavailability of the wing liferafts led the Board to question the advisability of their being externally stowed. Their unavailability can be attributed to the loss of the left wing and/or to the increase in inflation time resulting from the decrease in the temperature of the CO_2 after prolonged flight at high altitude.

It was learned that the survivors had considerable difficulty in finding the only available liferaft and in locating the other survivors while in the water. Consideration was given to improving the liferaft lighting systems so that in high seas, such as were encountered here, they could more easily be found. In addition, automatically activated lights should be required on all lifejackets.

The testimony of many of the survivors casts doubt on the adequacy of the inflation means for the lifejackets installed on this airplane. Many had considerable trouble inflating their jackets since they could not find the cartridge lanyard. There were also many reports of difficulty in swimming with the inflated jackets even though they had been previously checked for tightness by the stewardesses.

The report also observed the captain's choice of ditching heading, based on the wind and sea state information, was not in accord with the procedures outlined in the approved Flying Tiger Manual or with the procedures recommended by the U. S. Coast Guard or Air Sea Rescue Manuals. Captain Murray stated he chose a heading of 265 degrees magnetic to land into the wind. This was based on forecast information passed to him during his descent which indicated that the winds were approximately 25 knots from 260 degrees and the primary swell was from 260 degrees 8 to 12 feet in height.

When asked why he chose the ditching heading of 265 degrees magnetic, he said that he had been advised by Gander Radio that the primary swells were from 260 degrees and the winds were from 265 degrees at 30 knots. Directions given in forecasts such as these are headings and magnetic variation must be taken into account. The magnetic variation in the locale of the ditching is in excess of 20 degrees.

Captain Murray further testified that the sea was covered with white caps, but the primary swells were quite apparent and appeared to be 15 to 20 feet high, He stated that he was familiar with the ditching procedures in The Flying Tiger Line manual and was aware of the stipulation therein to never land into the face of a swell (or within 45 degrees of it). However, he stated that he did not agree with the ditching procedures in the manual concerning the direction of landing with respect to swell movement, and because of the distance between swells elected to land into the face of one.

Despite the foregoing, the CAB report included the following praise for Captain Murray:

"Under the circumstances of darkness, weather and high seas, which prevailed in the North Atlantic at the time of this ditching, the Board believes that the survival of 48 occupants of the aircraft was miraculous however, had lights been provided on the lifejackets even more persons might have survived."

It is the pilot's prerogative to choose the ditch heading. Fully aware of the accepted procedures Captain Murray made his choice and no one will ever know whether or not another heading would have made a difference. The next pilot chose a different path.

⌐⌐⌐

An Outstanding Feat
Northwest Airlines DC-7 Flight 293
Sitka Sound, Alaska

The Northwest Airlines Flight 293, a DC-7 four-engine aircraft, ditched near Biorka Island, Sitka Sound, Alaska, on October 22, 1962, about 12:52 P.M., Alaska Daylight Savings Time[50]. All 95 passengers and seven crew members successfully evacuated and were quickly rescued. No serious injuries were reported.

Flight 293 took off at 8:45 A.M., Pacific Daylight Savings Time, from McChord Air Force Base in Tacoma, Washington en route to Elmendorf Air Force Base in Anchorage, Alaska with Captain Vinton Hanson as pilot, Check Pilot Francis H. Kellogg[51], First Officer Earl C. Perry, Flight Engineer Donald E. Hackett, Steward Richard D. Chinnock, and Stewardesses Ruth E. Fullerton and Kathryn E. Ollinger.

Everything was normal at a cruising altitude of 14,000 feet until the craft reached the vicinity of Sandspit [Queen Charlotte Islands, British Columbia] when moderate icing was encountered. Flight 293 was given clearance to climb to 20,000 feet where the engineer officer proceeded to lean out the engines. The leaning of Number 1 engine had been completed and the engineer was working on Number 4 when there was a sudden loss of power on Number 2 engine.

After unsuccessful attempts for about 35 seconds to get power back on Number 2 with carburetor alcohol, carburetor heat and emergency enrichment, the propeller on Number 2 suddenly surged to 3400 to 3700 rpm and the crew was unable to feather the prop. The flight then declared an emergency, the first officer called "MAYDAY" four times on the emergency frequency of 121.5 megacycles, then gave a description of the emergency. Because of the intense noise of the prop, the first officer was unable to copy the first answer to his emergency call and because of the noise and static all communications had to be repeated several times.

The airplane was decelerated to 145 knots where it was found that the airplane stalled due to heavy icing and rolled to the right, so the descent was continued at 155 knots. Between 10,000 and 12,000 feet the engine froze. However, the propeller continued to rotate so the crew knew that it was only a matter of time before it would come off or the nose case would overheat and ignite, thus causing an uncontrollable fire.

Radio contact was made with the Coast Guard, FAA, Alaska Coastal Airlines and Sitka radio. Through these sources the crew was assured that there was no available landing field in the vicinity. The nearest suitable field was Gustavus, so it was decided to attempt to reach this field by way of Sitka. The crew was also informed that the weather ahead was clear. The flight broke out at 2,500 feet and continued to descend to 500 feet above sea level and about 25 miles off the coast of the Baranof Island.

Immediately upon hearing the runaway prop, Steward Chinnock went forward to the cockpit to receive orders from the flight crew.

He was told to evacuate the area around the runaway prop. People were moved back and sat four and five in each triple seat. This was done by removing the arm rests. Later, prior to impact, these people sat on the floor between seats with their backs to the outside bulkheads. There was no panic among the passengers; they did exactly as they were told. Several became ill from the combination of turbulence and the effect of the situation on their nerves.

All passengers were told to don their life jackets; the jackets from the evacuated areas were passed back to the people who had moved. Children were told to inflate their life jackets and adults warned not to inflate theirs until after leaving the ship. All loose articles were stowed in the lavatories, under seats and in empty berths.

The passengers were then told where the various exits were and also were told how to climb out with one shoulder and foot at the same time. Coats, pillows and blankets were passed out for padding and to wear after ditching.

There were some passengers who showed their fright more than others and they were given duties. Some were placed by the exits and were shown how to open the doors. A hand or a pat on the shoulder by crew members also had a psychological effect on some of the more restless passengers. All in all, however, they behaved beautifully. Cabin crew members sat on the floor between seats and out toward the aisle where the passengers could see them at all times. This seemed to help the morale of the passengers.

One passenger insisted upon opening the emergency exits before landing and throwing all loose articles. out. He also mistook the exhaust flame on No. 3 engine for fire and finally had to be quieted by Chinnock. A number of people were so frightened that they just sat in their seats stunned, but snapped out of it the minute someone would speak to them. They also seemed to relax some when, upon approaching the surface of the sea, they could see islands and could also see that the water was glassy smooth. The fact that it was daylight, too, was a great help for morale .

Coast Guard Air Station Annette Island learned of NWA 293's emergency about 10 minutes after Captain Hanson reported it, and as luck would have it, a Coast Guard Albatross aircraft was only 70 miles from the plane on a routine logistics mission. The aircraft commander, Lieutenant (LT) James Glasgow, immediately diverted to intercept. He rendezvoused with the troubled plane 17 miles west of Biorka Island at 12:45 P.M. Meanwhile the Coast Guard Cutter *Sorrel* (a 180-foot buoy tender) received a telephone call from the FAA tower in Sitka alerting her to the emergency. The cutter—believing at first that NWA 293 intended to ditch in Sitka Harbor—immediately launched a boat to clear the harbor of traffic. Moments later, however, orders came from the Coast Guard Search and Rescue Coordination Center in Juneau for *Sorrel* to get underway and at 1:00P.M. she did.

Fifteen miles southwest of Sitka lay Biorka Island, site of a USCG Loran-A station and an FAA communications station, both of which were regularly supplied from Sitka by an FAA supply boat appropriately named the *FEDAIR I*. This tough little boat was immediately dispatched to assist in rescuing survivors.

As rescue units raced to the scene, the pilots brought the aircraft down for her last landing. When the crippled aircraft was 15 or 20 feet above the water First Officer Kellogg fully extended the wing flaps and turned off all electrical power. Captain Hanson then ditched the aircraft on a heading of between 300 and 330 degrees at a speed of about 95 knots.

The landing was absolutely parallel to and on top of the swell, resulting in a perfect ditching. The Coast Guard crewmen in the Albatross flying directly overhead mentioned that the ditching looked to them like a beautiful seaplane landing.

Captain Hanson later recalled: "Knowing the direction of swells is imperative for a successful ditching. We should bear in mind that unless the wind is very strong (40 or 50 knots), the swell movement will determine the direction to ditch."

The landing was very smooth but deceleration was rapid. There were two impacts. Some witnesses claimed that the deceleration was no greater than full reverse thrust used to slow an aircraft during a normal landing. During impact the flight crew could see no spray and after coming to a stop there was no water in the windshields. The DC-7 floated well with a tail low position, as passengers had been moved from the forward area.

The time of ditching was 12:52 P.M.

After impact and after the emergency exits were opened, some water came into the cabin. It was approximately ankle deep at the wing exits and knee deep by the galley and main exit by the time all the passengers had left the plane. The cockpit, which remained high during evacuation was dry at all times.

Rafts were immediately launched; two over the wings, two through the main door and one through the back emergency exit. A 10-man raft was launched through the emergency exit of the cockpit. Some difficulty was encountered with the 10-man raft during handling, as the cover snaps were undone in pulling it out. The discharge handle and static lines were also snarled from handling, but the raft was finally ejected through the cockpit window and inflated by First Officer Perry. All other rafts opened perfectly.

In trying to slide into the raft from the cockpit, Captain Hanson missed the raft and was immersed in the water which was approximately 47 or 48 degrees Fahrenheit. A number of passengers who made exit through the rear emergency window also became wet since the tail was at an attitude that allowed water into the plane from this area. A very excited woman accidentally dropped her infant into the sea while transferring to the raft. The infant was quickly retrieved unharmed.

Within five minutes of the ditching, LT Glasgow in the Coast Guard Albatross landed with some difficulty in the area in a southwesterly direction across the swells. Shortly afterwards two Alaska Coastal-Ellis amphibians also landed nearby.

With great delicacy, LT Glasgow taxied over to the rafts and, making use of its prop blast, blew the rafts over to the FAA supply boat *FEDAIR I*. Twenty-four minutes after the ditching, with all personnel accounted for and safely on board the *FEDAIR I*, the DC-7 sank in 300 feet of water. *Sorrel* rendezvoused with *FEDAIR I* half an hour later and all 102 survivors were transferred from the overloaded supply boat to the cutter, for delivery to Sitka.

There were only minor injuries among the survivors: one passenger wrenched his back during the ditching, and another broke a toe while disembarking from the rafts of the *FEDAIR I*.

When interviewed by a reporter from the Sitka *Daily Sentinel*, Captain Hanson said about the ditching: "Everything was in our favor. Sea conditions and weather were with us", and regarding the evacuation, "the whole ship was evacuated in 2½ to 3 minutes."

Flight attendant Kathryn Ottinger reported that "there was no panic; all of the passengers did just exactly what we asked them to do."

Notwithstanding the matter-of-fact, professional tone of the flight crew, the Coast Guard and civil aviators who observed the ditching had nothing but superlatives for Captain Hanson's feat.

Interviewed in Ketchikan the next day, LT Glasgow said "The pilot of that aircraft did everything just right. The crew was real sharp. The passengers evacuated real fast. It was almost a classic", and noted that the scene was just like a training film he had seen showing rescue operations in ideal conditions.

The pilots of the Alaska Coastal-Ellis planes had similar comments, saying, "it was the finest ditching they had ever seen, even in filmed examples of how it should be done." The films they had seen may well have been those taken aboard *Ponchartrain* during the ditching of Pan Am *Sovereign of the Skies*, Flight 943.

Lessons Learned

The primary lesson derived from this ditching is that following all of the recommended ditching procedures significantly enhances the chances of survival.

Among these procedures which helped insure rescue vessels and aircraft were nearby was that immediately upon the event of the runaway prop, an emergency was declared and a "Mayday" call was made on the emergency frequency of 121.5 megacycles. The Coast Guard and the National Search and Rescue Manual both stress the importance of declaring an emergency as soon as possible to enable bearings to be taken on the airplane from land, sea, and air.

The reports mention that the passengers thanked their pre-flight briefing which is mandatory before over water flights. Everyone seemed to know his or her duties and evidently performed those duties in an expeditious manner. Another key point is that all reports indicate that there were few words spoken between all crew members and they all kept an outwardly calm demeanor.

An area not usually covered in the CAB reports is the psychological aspects of ditching. Post-ditching interviews revealed that the more physical activity in the cabin during the preparation for ditching the easier it was on the morale of the passengers. Talking on the Public Address System, assigning and reassigning passengers to various seats, checking on life jackets, and assigning duties to various passengers so that other passengers could hear, kept the passengers from thinking of themselves and also had a calming effect from the knowledge that the crew members knew what they were doing.

The official Civil Aeronautics Board's report noted that "the successful ditching at sea of the DC-7 and the evacuation of all 95 passengers and seven crew members without injury is, under any circumstances, an outstanding feat."

7. Faith, Birds, and Hijacking

Other Ditching Causes

We've seen how mechanical problems, unforeseen weather conditions, and faulty navigation have caused ditchings. However, three ditchings have unique causes. One was based on faith, another by too many birds, and the third was a hijacking that went tragically wrong.

Faith

Faith in a divine being helps many people get through difficult and dangerous situations, but belief alone isn't always enough. Sometimes it needs to be assisted by personal action. This was the case on August 6, 2005, when Tuninter Flight 1153 ditched in the Mediterranean Sea north of Sicily with 39 people on board.

A short time after takeoff from Bari, Italy, the aircraft's two engines slowed to a halt, even though the gauges showed fuel remaining for the flight. Instead of attempting to glide the aircraft to a safe landing at the nearest airport in Palermo, Italy, the pilot, Captain Chafik Gharby, prayed to Allah and his Prophet, Muhammad to save him and his passengers, but he didn't take any other actions.

The aircraft broke up on impact, killing 16 passengers. Twenty-three survivors swam for their lives, and some of them managed to live by clinging to a piece of the fuselage that stayed afloat.

The investigation revealed that the fuel indicator was reading incorrectly because it was designed to fit into a smaller plane. Contributing to the loss of life was the fact that a high-wing aircraft allows for less evacuation time because the wings do not provide flotation until the fuselage has disappeared beneath the surface.

At first, Captain Chafik Gharby was hailed as a hero for having saved the lives of most of the passengers. However, after the investigation an Italian court charged him, his co-pilot, and several Tuninter executives and technicians with a range of offences, including manslaughter.

The judges accepted the prosecution's case that the pilot, instead of making a crash landing on the sea, should have been able to glide the plane to nearby Palermo airport. In cockpit recordings entered as evidence he was heard calling for the help of "Allah and Muhammad his prophet".

Gharby was sentenced to 10 years in jail for failing to take emergency measures which would have avoided the crash.

In addition, the co-pilot, Ali Kebaier, also received a 10-year sentence. Tuninter's director-general, Moncef Zouari, and the company's technical director were both given nine years. A mechanic and two executives in the airline's maintenance department each received eight-year sentences.[52]

In this case faith, unsupported by personal action was not enough to save the aircraft, many of the passengers or, ultimately, the pilots.

Birds

Although there are hundreds of collisions between aircraft and birds (bird strikes) reported each year, few prove fatal to the aircraft and only one has caused a ditching. According to the FAA National Wildlife Strike Database, since 1960, 26 large-transport aircraft have been destroyed because of bird strikes worldwide. Ninety-three percent of these strikes occurred during takeoff or landing at an altitude of about 500 feet above ground level or less when the airplane was still near an airport.

The greatest loss of life directly linked to a bird strike was on October 4, 1960. An Eastern Air Lines Flight 375, a Lockheed L-188 Electra, taking off from Boston's Logan Airport flew through a flock of common starlings, damaging all four engines. The plane crashed shortly after take-off into Boston harbor, with 62 fatalities out of 72 passengers. Subsequently, minimum bird ingestion standards for jet engines were developed by the FAA.

Birds put Chuck Martin's flying to the test in the late 1970s. This time he was captaining a Delta Airlines DC-8 jet airliner on a routine flight to Tampa. While making his landing approach, a flock of ducks flew into the jet's path. At a combined speed of almost 250 knots some of the waterfowl were sucked into the engines while others punched holes in the wings and smashed the cockpit windshield. Too late and too low to declare an emergency, Chuck landed the damaged aircraft and taxied to the gate with superb aplomb. Chuck considered what happened just another day at the office. Ironically, it was the first day of Duck Season.

The only ditching attributed to these fowl collisions was US Airways Flight 1549 on January 15, 2009. According to information from the National Transportation Safety Board Report both engines were operating normally until they each ingested at least two large birds weighing about 8 pounds each which caused mechanical damage that in turn prevented the engines from being able to provide sufficient thrust to sustain flight.

If the engines' electronic control system had been capable of informing the flight crew about the continuing operational status of the engines, the flight crew would have been aware that thrust could not be restored and would not have spent valuable time trying to relight the engines. [53]

In addition to the geese, there were five serious injuries and 95 other people were treated for minor injuries and hypothermia. The lack of fatalities or a greater number of serious injuries is surprising, given that there was less than two minutes of warning before impact.

Unlike most of the other ditchings where the majority of passengers had flotation devices when they exited the aircraft, in this one only about 10 passengers retrieved life vests after impact and evacuated with them. Of the remaining 140 passengers about 77 retrieved flotation seat cushions before leaving the plane.

It is remarkable that everyone survived on board US Airways Flight 1549 given the short time between the warning and the impact and the overall lack of preparedness.

On a final note about bird strikes, according the NTSB, the Hudson River accident was not a typical bird-strike event; therefore, this accident demonstrates that a bird strike does not need to be typical to be hazardous.

Hijacked

Over the years most hijackings have been perpetrated by people seeking political asylum or by terrorists wanting publicity and ransom. In the 1970s hijackings seemed to take place almost weekly. Between 1947 and 2009 there were 78 reported hijackings. Fortunately, most of the time no one was injured or killed, but this was not always the case.

The first recorded aircraft hijacking on February 21, 1931, in Arequipa, Peru was motivated by politics. Byron Rickards, flying a Pan American Airways Ford Tri-Motor aircraft, was approached on the ground by armed revolutionaries. He refused to fly them anywhere and was locked up. After a ten day stand-off Rickards was informed that the revolution was successful and they would release him in return for flying one of their number to Lima.[54,55]

It was in July 1947 that the next and the world's first fatal hijacking took place when three Romanians killed the pilot during a flight from Romania to Turkey.[56]

The first attempted hijacking of a commercial airliner reportedly happened on July 16, 1948 and was solely for the purpose of robbing those on board. The *Miss Macao*, a Catalina amphibian, was on a routine flight from Macau to Hong Kong. She was hijacked a few minutes after take off by four men, three armed with guns, one of whom demanded that the pilot surrender the controls. The pilot, Dale Warren Cramer, refused and the co-pilot attacked one of the intruders with a flag-post rod. In the confusion, Cramer was shot dead and collapsed onto the flight controls. The plane went into an uncontrolled dive and crashed into the sea, killing 25 of the 26 people aboard. The sole survivor, Huang Yu, later confessed to being one of the hijackers.

From this point on all except one of the hijackings ended on land. The one exception was on November 23, 1996, when Ethiopian

Airlines Flight 961, en route from Addis Ababa to Nairobi, was hijacked by three Ethiopians seeking political asylum. The plane ditched after running out of fuel. Only 50 of the 175 passengers and crew on board survived. Although Flight 961 is not the deadliest hijacking in history, it is the deadliest ditching.[57]

꧁꧂

Ethiopian Airlines Boeing 767-260ER
"I thought I had finished my life."[58]

Takahiko Sugiyama

On November 23, 1996, Ethiopian Airlines Flight 961 was en route from Addis Ababa, Ethiopia to Nairobi, Kenya. The aircraft carried 163 passengers and 12 crew members from more than 35 nations. The hijacking occurred at approximately 11:20 A.M. (ZULU) in Ethiopian airspace.

Approximately 20 minutes into the flight, the three Ethiopian males separately approached the cockpit from the rear of the aircraft. At least two of them had been in the lavatory before the aircraft took off. One of the men ran down the aisle toward the cockpit shouting statements that could not be understood, and his two accomplices followed soon after. The hijackers were described as young (mid-twenties), inexperienced, psychologically fragile, and intoxicated. They were clean shaven and dressed in Western clothes, and one wore a black stocking cap which covered his face.

When the three men reached the cockpit, one or more of them forced their way in.

The pilot, Captain Luel Abate remembers: "[The hijackers] knew they wouldn't make it to Australia—they just wanted us to crash. They should be dead. The way they were talking they didn't want to live."

Ethiopian passenger Bisrat Alemu recalls: "They said, `We escaped from prison. We are against the government. We are hijacking the plane. We have an explosive. If anybody moves, we'll explode it,' "

Four hours later the plane was nearly out of fuel as it approached the Comoros islands.

The pilot then made the first of only two communications to the passengers during the ordeal, informing them of the fuel shortage and the loss of an engine.

His further instructions were to maintain calm and prepare for an emergency landing by securely putting on, but not inflating, life jackets. The reaction of the passengers to these instructions ranged from calm to panic. In the business class section, the search for life jackets was initiated by a passenger. While the flight attendants assisted those who were distraught, the passenger located the life jackets in an unmarked metal box lying between the seats and assisted in distributing them.

The plane continued to lose altitude and began to sway. Much of this time was consumed by instructions being exchanged between passengers and crew on proper use of the life jackets. Despite the crew's instructions, sounds of life jackets being inflated could be heard throughout the aircraft.

Soon after his first communication to the passengers, Abate made his second and final announcement instructing passengers to assume a pre-crash position. This involved their bending forward with pillows on their heads in order to brace for a hard landing. The passengers' reactions were the same as earlier, varying from calm to panic. At least one flight attendant prayed on the floor and a father held three children in his lap. The pilot signed off by stating that the passengers knew the hijackers were responsible and implied that if the hijackers survived, the passengers would be able to identify them.

Abate's co-pilot, Yonas Mekuria, had been attacked with an axe shortly after the hijackers took over the cockpit, but he remained in his seat, assisting Abate. The hijackers ignored Abate's plea to land at the Comoros's Prince Said Ibrahim International Airport, and instead, one of them, drinking a bottle of whiskey, decided to fly the plane himself.

When the plane ran out of fuel, both engines failed. Abate and Mekuria, bleeding and bruised, fought with the hijackers. Abate used the ram air turbine to preserve the aircraft's most essential functions, but in this mode some hydraulic systems—such as the flaps—were inoperative. Electricity was out and the cabin became dark and quiet. The plane was approaching the Comoros Islands. Abate had been given clearance to land at Moroni Airport, Grand Comoro, but he knew the plane would not reach it. He tried to land the plane in the water near the Galawa seaside resort.

The hijackers, however, realizing that they had failed, attempted to take control of the instruments. They wanted to turn the hijacking into a suicide mission by crashing into the resort. The struggle in the cockpit between the pilot and a hijacker was evident as the aircraft, gliding at 200 miles per hour without flaps down, approached the water. It hit at more than 175 knots (about 200 miles per hour or 320 kilometers per hour).

Franklin Huddle, then U.S. consul general in Bombay, and his wife, Chanya Huddle, were headed for vacation near Nairobi.

"It's interesting what goes through your mind when the plane goes down," he said during an interview. "At the last second, my wife suggested eating a peanut-butter sandwich because we might not eat for a while after we were rescued. I'm a former pilot so I know what it's like to ditch planes over water. I thought we were going to go down for the count," Huddle recalled later.

The left engine and wingtip struck the water first, causing the plane to overturn at least once and break into three segments 500 yards off Le Galawa Beach Hotel near Mitsamiouli at the northern end of Grand Comoro Island and 16 miles from Moroni Airport.

There were screams as the plane hit the water, a deafening explosion as the cabin broke up, then a few seconds of silence.

One passenger, Takahiko Sugiyama, blacked out when the plane slammed into the sea and broke into three pieces. "I think I must have lost consciousness," Sugiyama said. "Then I felt the water coming in. I realized I was alive."

"I was afraid of sharks," he said with a laugh that made him wince from his chest wounds. "I could see the beach, and I was sure then I would be rescued."

Huddle said that he and his wife were popped out into the water: "The plane basically broke apart. I was swimming in the water with a foot that was basically flayed in half."

The majority of the survivors hung onto the fuselage section, which was floating; the rear section of the plane was submerged. Many victims were killed as a direct result of the impact. Others drowned because their inflated life jackets prevented them from swimming out of the water-filled fuselage. The pilot and copilot survived, the hijackers did not.

Because Captain Abate managed to bring the airliner down so close to shore, tourists and island residents were able to reach the survivors quickly. When Sugiyama struggled out of the aircraft, rescuers already had surrounded the jet. Some passengers managed to swim to shore on their own. In addition, several boats and small vessels were immediately sent from the resort to the crash site.

The resort's open air restaurant was turned into a triage station staffed by ten vacationing French and South African doctors, and the patients were later sent to Moroni Hospital. Recovered bodies were zipped into dark bags and hauled to an ambulance for transport to a makeshift morgue set up in a former government meat warehouse.

Adding to the tragedy, a number of the locals looted not only the wreckage but also some of the victims.

Amazingly, a video captured the plane's fatal descent. It was shot by a South African couple who witnessed the crash as they sunned themselves on the beach of their honeymoon hotel in the Comoros. The wife began filming the low-flying plane because she and her husband thought it was an air show for tourists.[59]

Lessons Learned

Apparently there weren't any that came out of this disaster although Flight 961 was one of the deadliest hijackings in history. From

1990—1995, ten hijackings took place in Ethiopia by Ethiopians seeking political asylum and escape from poverty conditions in their country. But, only one injury resulted from these hijackings and all the hijackers surrendered to authorities when the incidents were safely over. Flight 961 was significant in that it validated a continued threat to civil aviation in a region where air carrier activity had increased substantially in recent years. The threat against air carriers in the area was also heightened by the hijackers' change to lethal acts not demonstrated in previous incidents.

However, no significant changes were instituted to airline security due to this event nor would there be until after the September 11, 2001 attacks in the U.S.

8. Pan American Sovereign of the Skies

"Just in Case"

Pan American World Airways Flight 943, a Boeing 377, ditched in the Pacific Ocean near Ocean Station November (located between Honolulu and San Francisco) on October 16, 1956, at 6:15 A.M. There were 24 passengers aboard., including three infants, and a flight crew of seven. All 31 occupants were evacuated safely; the aircraft sank in deep water and could not be recovered.[60]

Aloha

The *Sovereign* had recently arrived from the Orient as part of an around the world trip and was finally headed back to her home base in San Francisco. Her flight crew that night included veteran Captain Richard N. Ogg, First Officer George L. Haaker, Navigator Richard L. Brown, Flight Engineer Frank Garcia Jr., Purser Patricia Reynolds, Stewardess Mary Ellen "Len" Daniel, and Stewardess Katherine S. Araki.

Among the passengers were Richard and Jane Gordon travelling with their two-and-a half year old twin girls Maureen and Elizabeth. The family was returning from Richard's tour of duty as the Provincial Public Affairs Officer at Iloilo City in the Philippines. Other passengers included US Navy Commander Kenneth Strickler; sixteen-year-old Paul Bird; Dr. Marcel Touzé, a French Army surgeon returning to France on vacation after three years in Indochina; two middle-aged California ladies, Mrs. Ruby Danu and Mrs. Louise Walker, each traveling alone; Tjong Soen Lie, from Djakarta, Indonesia; and the Dutch businessman Hendrik Braat. Mrs. Rebecca Jacobe, from the Philippines was travelling with her three-year-old daughter Joanne and two fellow Filipinos Dr. Cleto Cortes and Dr. Manuel Pangan.

In planning the flight, Captain Ogg and his crew listened as dispatcher Denis Sunderland briefed them on the flight plan. For the first half of the trip they would fly at an altitude of 13,000 feet. At the halfway point, almost over Weather Station November and the Coast Guard Cutter *Ponchartrain*, they were to climb to 21,000 feet. Sunderland read off the weather conditions they might expect—at San Francisco, at Sacramento, the alternate landing area, and at Honolulu, should a return become necessary. He also told them the conditions they would probably find at sea level if they had to ditch.

As the passengers boarded the plane, they were greeted by the two stewardesses, Len Daniel and Katherine Araki. Len ushered the 11 first-class passengers into their section, back of the wings and separated from the tourist class by a bulkhead. Katherine showed the 13 tourist-class passengers to their seats in the forward section, directly behind the cockpit and extending halfway back over the wings.

At 8:26 P.M., Honolulu time, Captain Ogg gently lifted *Sovereign* from the runway and turned her past Diamond Head, into the darkening eastern sky on a heading for San Francisco. The flight plan called for a flight of eight hours and 54 minutes, leveling off initially at 13,000 feet, and then, just prior to the midway point, climbing to 21,000 feet for the remainder of the trip. The engines sang a reassuring song as they settled down into the cruise portion of the flight.

The weather was good and the air smooth. Navigation Officer Brown would have no problem locating his favorite stars this evening.

Prior to takeoff Purser Pat Reynolds made her routine announcement over the cabin loud-speakers: "Good evening, ladies and gentlemen. Welcome aboard Strato-Clipper 943. Your stewardesses, Miss Araki and Miss Daniel are now going to demonstrate the type of life jacket carried aboard this plane."

Paul Bird, who had boarded the plane in Tokyo, turned to his seat companion, Hendrik Braat, and said, "Oh, no! Do we have to go through all this again?"

Over the loud-speakers, Pat Reynolds continued: "...a pamphlet entitled Emergency Instructions, please read at your earliest convenience."

Stewardesses Len Daniel and Katherine Araki showed the passengers where to locate and how to put on their "Mae West" life jackets. In addition, they provided each passenger with a folder describing ditching procedures entitled "Just in Case."

As soon as the *No Smoking* sign went out, some of the first-class passengers walked down the spiral staircase to the lower-deck cocktail lounge.

By the time *Sovereign of the Skies* reached her initial cruising altitude of 13,000 feet, the stewardesses were ready to serve dinner. But just then the *Sovereign* ran into a layer of heavy cumulus clouds and the flight became unpleasantly bumpy. Conditions were so bad that some of the passengers became airsick and Pat Reynolds postponed the dinner.

Making her way forward to the cockpit, she spoke to Captain Ogg. "How long is this going to last?" she asked. "I want to get dinner over so my passengers can retire." Ogg, looking out over a fluffy gray field of clouds, some directly in the path of the plane, others towering on either side of it, said, "I don't know, Pat, but I think we'll be out of this stuff pretty soon."

When the air smoothed out, Len Daniel began laying out the trays with the "Aloha Champagne Supper." For the first-class passengers the menu included Rock Cornish Game Hens with Wild Rice Farci, a choice of Belgian Spring Carrots or Baby Brussels Sprouts and Champagne Brut-Almaden. The tourist-class passengers were served Braised Sirloin Tips for their entrée. They could buy wines and liquors if they wanted to.

After dinner the cabin lights were dimmed and the passengers settled in for the night. Pillows and blankets were handed out to those in Tourist Class while the First Class passengers moved aft to their Pullman-style berths. By a little after midnight, San Francisco time—

two hours after leaving Honolulu—dinner was over and Flight 943's passengers settled down for the night.

Because only 13 people were traveling tourist class in a section designed to carry 35, the passengers were able to take advantage of the extra space. By removing the intervening seat arms, the passengers were able to stretch out full length.

Bidding Mrs. Walker "Good night," Mrs. Dami left her assigned seat, took off her earrings, and stretched out on two seats with her feet resting against the glass of one of the windows.

Ocean Station November

As the *Sovereign* headed east that evening, Coast Guard Cutter *Pontchartrain* was beginning her third and last week on Ocean Station November. The patrol had gone well with excellent weather and numerous swim calls. Interest generated by the World Series between the New York Yankees and Brooklyn Dodgers [the Yankees won 4 games to 3], and the opening of the football season had helped.

Drills had been frequent with both day and night ditch and rescue emphasized. Quarterly gunnery exercises were conducted along with man over-board drills using both the pulling boats and the Motor Whale boats. The Combat Information Center (CIC) gang had worked with 776 planes and were talking of a possible record for numbers of aircraft handled on a single patrol.

In the wardroom, the cutter's captain, Commander Bill Earle, was playing bridge. He and his partner, Lieutenant Commander John McCurdy, the chief engineer, were once again trouncing Lieutenant Commander Bill Kesler, the executive officer, and Ensign Dick Abrahams.

Bill Earle preferred duty on the rougher Atlantic. "It presents much more of a challenge." he had once told civilian weatherman Ray Valente. But tonight he was feeling good on this, his first patrol in the Pacific.

On the deck, many of the crew were watching Rory Calhoun in the movie "Powder River."

In his bunk, the Ponchartrain's cook, nineteen-year-old Bill Simpson, was curled up with a paperbound book—George Gamow's *Birth and Death of the Sun*. He had just reached the chapter explaining the construction of the atom.

Nearby, fireman Brad Endersbe rooted through a pile of paperbacks. He had read all except one: *Barbary Slave*, by Kevin Matthews. He smiled at the blurb on the back. "Sold into slavery...It was unthinkable that innocent Eve Doremus of Boston would be forced to parade her naked beauty in a Barbary Coast slave mart..."

As Endersbe climbed into his hunk to learn more about Eve, he hoped that the captain wouldn't call a practice ditching drill, as he had the previous night. It was 10:26 P.M., San Francisco time.

Runaway

Sovereign cruised into the night at 13,000 feet until close to the midpoint of their Pacific crossing, when their clearance to the final level of 21,000 feet was approved by Air Traffic Control. Garcia set the engines at climb power, and the plane climbed easily upward to the new level. In a few moments they leveled off, and the crew once more allowed the aircraft to increase speed, settling into the routine for the final pull to San Francisco.

At precisely 3:23 A.M. the soles of Mrs. Dami's feet, planted against the plane's window, began to tingle. The sensation surged up her legs and she awoke in terror, her whole body shaking violently. In the darkened cabin everything seemed to be "shaking to pieces." The nightmare was accentuated by the high, harsh whine of a propeller gone berserk.

Len Daniel had just stepped onto the flight deck to take coffee orders from the crew as First Officer Haaker called for cruise power, and Frank Garcia began easing the throttles back from the climb setting. Suddenly the calm on the flight deck was shattered by a shrill high-pitched whine and the airplane lurched to one side, almost knocking Len off her feet. Lee Haaker felt the controls vibrate.

A quick glance at the engine instruments told the crew the bad news: the prop on the number 1 engine was running away. Haaker saw that the engine RPMs were rapidly approaching the upper limit; it was over 2900 on the gauge, and he quickly pushed the feathering button to bring it under control. At the same time he slowed the huge Boeing and lowered the flaps 30 degrees.

This was the "book" solution to the problem; at the lower speed the propeller would be easier to control. Frank Garcia, meanwhile, shut off the fuel to the number 1 engine, and pulled back the throttles on the other three to help slow the airplane. Unfortunately nothing seemed to help. The needle on the number 1 tachometer hit the upper limit of the gauge and stayed there. They had a true runaway. Unlike a damaged engine which could be stopped and the propeller feathered into a minimum drag configuration, a runaway acted like a flat plate disk out there in the slipstream, creating terrible drag.

Richard Gordon recalls: "At that moment I was sound asleep in a berth in the rear section of the plane. Jane, who could not sleep, was in a berth directly behind mine with the two children. Suddenly I was awakened by a frighteningly loud and eerie noise that shook the plane. I poked my head out of the berth to see what was wrong. Jane, previously awake, was in the aisle beckoning furiously to me to get dressed."

Captain Ogg had been sitting at the navigator's station when the engine went rogue. Quickly regaining the left seat, his first action was to radio the *Ponchartrain*. At the time, *Sovereign of the Skies* was less than forty miles from the cutter. Ogg motioned to Haaker to radio the cutter.

Pontchartrain

On board *Ponchartrain* the mid-watch (12:00—4:00 A.M.) was winding down and Quartermaster Third Class Irvin Laxineta was making his final entries into the log. The Officer Of the Deck, Lt. (jg) James Frost, had instructed the Boatswains Mate of the Watch Richard "Dick" Olson to wake the next watch standers. Suddenly an urgent voice broke through the darkness:

"Bridge—Combat. We have an aircraft, 40 miles from this station, reporting a runaway engine!"

Frost stepped into the Combat Information Center (CIC), to get amplifying information. Sonarman Third Class Fred Holmes, reported nothing further heard from Pan Am 943.

"Ask him if he desires assistance from this station, or if he requests a communication alert be initiated."

These words came back from the pilot, spoken in a calm, restrained tone.

"This is Clipper 943. We are having emergency engine trouble. May have to ditch. Please alert your crew and stand by to assist us."

"Roger your message, Clipper 943. Will give you continuous beacon. Our crew is being alerted."

Frost told Laxineta to notify Commander Earle of the emergency. He then sent the messenger to wake up the communications officer and the operations officer, according to distress procedures.

Again the pilot's voice: "I will definitely have to ditch. Did you hear? I definitely have to ditch."

This message came over loud and clear to CIC down below. Immediately thereafter, the general alarm was sounded, and the word was going out over the public address system (1MC).

"ALL HANDS, MAN YOUR DITCH AND RESCUE STATIONS. THIS IS NO DRILL. THERE IS A PLANE IN THE AREA THAT WILL HAVE TO DITCH."

With the alarm still sounding, men all over the ship started jumping out of their bunks, hastily putting on clothing, and running to their stations. Even though the crew members were fully prepared and intensively trained the dreaded D-word rang an ominous tone.

Another communiqué: "This is Clipper 943. I'm losing altitude fast. I'm coming in on your beacon and will try to make it to the ship. Can you give me a recommended ditch heading?"

The CIC Officer, who had now assumed duty as Air Controller as per the standard Ditch and Rescue organization, responded immediately with the currently posted ditch heading and assured the plane's pilot that they were alerting all hands and would be ready to assist.

The Air Controller worked with Captain Ogg according to the standard Ditch and Rescue Information sheet, exchanging all necessary information relative to ditching. The calculations were quickly computed and the ditching heading was set for 245 degrees true. A previously prepared Ditch Check-off List was followed in a flurry of organized activity with only minutes to go before the ditching was to take place.

Basic Ditch & Rescue stations were manned by 3:30 and 24-inch searchlights were orbited overhead. Boat number 4, the Motor Whale boat, was manned and made ready for lowering. Deck rescue gear and liferafts were being broken out. Electric waterlights were being brought up to the fantail.

The aircraft passed overhead during this period and Captain Ogg announced he would go off and dump gasoline. Mortar flare illumination was secured and the laying of electric waterlights on the ditch heading was commenced. Since it was apparent there would not be enough time to rig electric water lights for a quick ditching, Mk II carbide lights were called for.

Meanwhile, Captain Ogg had changed his mind about dumping gasoline and instead made a practice run up the ditch patch at about 2,000 feet altitude.

All Through the Night

Having done all they could for the time being, a sense of calm returned in the cockpit. The aircraft had been in a slow descent as they headed toward the *Ponchartrain*, the crew trying several times to unsuccessfully feather the uncooperative prop on the No. 1 engine.

Ogg finally told Garcia to cut off the oil to the engine in hopes that it would eventually seize, stopping the prop.

With a sudden jarring thud the propeller uncoupled from the "frozen" engine and, now free, began to wind-mill. The noise and vibration stopped, but now they still had the drag of the propeller to contend with.

At 5,000 feet they added power to level off and received another surprise, one that effectively sealed the fate of the unlucky *Sovereign*. The No. 4 outboard engine on the opposite wing was not responding and would only run at about half power. The vital signs were all pretty close to normal, it just wouldn't produce the power. The crew discovered that they could keep the airplane in the air with rated power on the inboards, and partial power on No. 4.

They also found that if they slowed to 140 knots the problem prop out there on No. 1 was just barely controllable at the upper limit of the tachometer, but 140 knots was about 20 knots below efficient two engine cruise speed. There was finality to it: they were facing the ultimate horror of trans-ocean flying: a ditching at sea.

Dick Gordon picks up the narrative:

"In a few moments, Captain Richard W. Ogg's cool, clear voice came over the loud speaker: 'Ladies and gentlemen, I'm sorry to wake you, but we have a real emergency. One of our engines is giving us some difficulty. Just in case we have to ditch the plane, please put on your life Jackets, take your seats, and fasten your seat belts.'

The next few minutes were probably the most trying for everyone on the plane. The experience was hard for me to believe. This was the sort of thing that heretofore 'always happened to the other fellow.'"

"I was brought back to reality by the screams of our children. We had to wake them to put their life jackets on, and they were not in the least understanding. At this point I couldn't keep myself from trembling."

The forty miles separating the *Sovereign* and *Pontchartrain* quickly disappeared and it wasn't long before the crew sighted *Ponchartrain*, it was a bright clear night and visibility was good.

The CIC Officer, who had now assumed duty as Air Controller as per the standard Ditch and Rescue organization, responded immediately with the currently posted ditch heading and assured Captain Ogg that the *Pontchartrain* would be ready to assist him.

Five minutes later, with the *Sovereign* only about five miles away, it was evident that there would be no time to lay a waterlight path or to fire a starshell barrage. Commander Earle ordered "Illuminate to starboard by mortar flares." The cutter was then on the recommended ditch heading moving at 10 knots.

Meanwhile, Captain Ogg, doing his own calculations, determined there was a large amount of fuel on board and he could hold his 2,000-foot altitude without too much difficulty. So he would try to postpone the ditching until daylight. Landing a plane on the ocean under any condition is terrifying, but at night, with only artificial illumination, it would be doubly so.

Now there was more time for both the *Sovereign* and *Ponchartrain* crews to review and be ready for every contingency. While the *Sovereign* was making eight-mile loops around the cutter, the two captains kept going over the procedures.

Captain Ogg and Frank Garcia turned the controls over to Lee Haaker and went aft to see to the preparations in the cabin. Pat Reynolds and her crew had already gone through the aisle and briefed their charges; Ogg and Haaker wanted to be sure that everyone knew how to handle the over-wing exits and the escape lines. Ogg later remarked on how calm everyone was, it was almost becoming a non-event.

One concern that he had was the placement of the passengers in seats over the wings. Captain Ogg was aware of the Pan Am Flight 845 incident the year before, in which a Boeing 377's tail section had broken off in a water landing.

He said later: "Because past Stratocruiser ditchings have shown a consistent history of tail separation, I instructed Purser Reynolds to remove all passengers from the last three rows of seats [these are aft of the wing]. Passengers were also removed from the vicinity of number 1 propeller."

Len Daniel recalls: "And so began for us, the attendants, a terribly busy time of making sure all items in the galley at the rear of the plane were tossed downstairs into the small bar area. On impact we didn't want oven pans flying through the cabin. Also all items in the overhead racks were emptied. This emergency happened at about 3:30 a.m. We showed passengers how to put on their lifejackets, reminding them not to inflate them until outside of the cabin.

"We designated certain people to help with opening window exits and main cabin doors. The extra engineer, who was new in this division, was going to help me in opening the main cabin door and launching the life raft located there."

During the long wait for daylight, Captain Ogg switched the seat-belt sign off and further briefed the passengers on what the plans were for ditching. Then he added: "By the way, there's nothing to worry about—the temperature of the water is 74 degrees and the Coast Guardsmen tell me they went swimming yesterday. So relax now and enjoy a cigarette."

The captain's words brought immediate relief to the passengers—even though they all knew that the decision was merely a temporary reprieve. In the hours that passed they talked, prayed and remembered—they'd started the trip as strangers and now they were drawn together by a common danger.

Dr. Touzé, looking out the window at the feathered propeller of No. 4 engine, was coldly realistic about their chances of survival. He believed that the impact would kill many. For himself, he didn't mind dying. but he had a horror of being crippled. He expected that many on board would suffer broken hips where the seat belts crossed the body as well as broken backs and fractured skulls. He decided that when the time came he would fasten his seat belt just above his hips.

Three passengers dozed. The stewardesses jokingly offered to pass out the magazines. A passenger wanted to know when breakfast would be served which got laughs from some of the passengers.

One factor that may have contributed greatly to the passengers' calmness in this emergency was Captain Ogg walking back once and talking to most of them personally.

"I told them that it would be easy and that I had no fear myself and that they, therefore, had no reason to be alarmed themselves. Also Mr. Haaker and Mr. Garcia and Mr. Brown visited the cabin at times and talked to the passengers. The passengers since told me that these visits back to the cabin were very helpful in making them feel confident we could get down okay."

"Jane and I spent most of this time in our seats with the children asleep in our laps," says Dick Gordon. "We calmed down enough to ask a barrage of questions of the young lady purser and the two stewardesses, who did everything possible to reassure and assist us. We were perplexed because there seemed to be no precise instructions for holding small children at the time of impact. We finally devised our own system by straddling our arms around each child and then holding tight to the seat bottoms.

"We did not talk very much to each other except occasionally to pray. Despite our anxiety, Jane and I both felt that we would come out of our ordeal safely. This, of course, was a measure of our faith in God and in our extremely competent crew."

Further ditching information was passed out during this period. The aircraft evacuation plan was carefully discussed, including matters of opening windows from the outside, where to chop into the fuselage if that should prove necessary, how passengers and crew members would debark, what equipment would be in the cutter's boats, how the children would be handled, and where in relation to the ditch path the plane should touch down.

Broken Tail and Hot Coffee

At first light, around 6:30 A.M., Commander Earle radioed Captain Ogg: "Good morning, Captain. It's a beautiful day down here. The easterly swells have increased a bit and I suggest we now shift to 330 degrees as a heading. We are prepared to mark out a landing path on this new heading with fire extinguisher foam whenever you want it."

Captain Ogg responded "We're all ready up here. My gals have done a great job and the passengers are quite calm. I think I'll wait until my gasoline is almost gone to reduce the chance of fire. This will probably be in about an hour but I'll give you plenty of advance warning." Commander Earle advised Captain Ogg that they would be having breakfast together before long and then asked how he liked his eggs.

By 7:00 it was broad daylight. *Pontchartain* left her station one-half mile beyond the end of the water light path and came to the new agreed upon ditch heading 330 degrees.

At 7:40 A.M., Captain Ogg radioed he would ditch at about 8:25 A.M. The *Pontchartrain* got underway at full speed and laid a two-mile-long foam path on the ditch heading to aid the pilot's depth perception. The cutter's crew began scrambling into boats, hauling rubber life rafts up to the rail, and putting Jacob's ladders over the side. Swimmers and deck rescue details were standing by. While this was going on, the plane made a practice run and reported the foam path clearly visible.

With his fuel nearly gone Captain Ogg circled to begin his last run. All preparations had been made. This was the real one.

Commander Earle's last radio words to Captain Ogg were: "You just set her down nice and easy, as close to us as possible, and we'll have you out in no time. Good luck and God bless you!"

Captain Ogg replied: "We have full confidence in you."

The pilots headed down the foam-marked path at 90 knots. Behind them in the passenger compartment they heard the sound of children crying. Normal procedure is for pilot and copilot to share landings and takeoffs. Now, in the cockpit. Haaker spoke to Ogg: "Dick, this is my landing."

Captain Ogg said, "Lee, let's make it together."

When the plane was a few feet above the water, Ogg dropped her in. She slid smoothly at first then bounced hard and whipped around violently as an engine tore loose. The sound of children crying was replaced by that of crushing metal and water rushing in.

In the plane's cabin, Hendrik Braat felt his seat belt break. Commander Strickler's side of the seat went up, swung to the right and his head smashed down on the arm of the chair. Mrs. Walker felt water spraying onto her. She looked up—and suddenly she was kicked in the head by Dr. Pangan, who sailed over her and landed several seats away on his face. Behind Pat Reynolds, the Clipper's big tail snapped off.

Len Daniel, jolted around in her seat, thought in despair, "We're turning over; how will we get them out?"

But no one screamed or cried, the plane's motion finally stopped and there was an instant of utter silence.

Frank Garcia remembers: "I saw the water spray over the windshield then felt a force pulling me into the seat and noticed the first officer's control column going back and forth. After that I saw nothing but water covering the windshield, and as soon as it started to recede I knew we were OK. After opening the cockpit door I got a shock when all I saw at the back of the aircraft was the Pacific Ocean.

Captain Ogg and his officers survived without injury. "I remember that there was one slight impact first, followed quickly by a very heavy impact during which Mr. Haaker and I were thrown forward and to the right. The airplane's nose was momentarily below the surface of the water. Then it bobbed to the surface and stopped. I remember a little water slopped over our feet at the time of the impact but it disappeared and there was no water on the flight deck when the airplane came to rest. The engineer ascertained that neither of us was hurt and we removed our safety belts and evacuated the crew compartment of the airplane.

"We found the door between the crew compartment and the passenger cabin to be jammed shut, but we didn't waste any time trying to open it because the Dutch door part was open allowing us easy access through into the passenger cabin. When we reached the passenger cabin the crew back there had already opened the main cabin door and had thrown out a raft which was being inflated at the time. The passengers were most orderly.

"None was hysterical or excited. They were lined up to get aboard the raft. Mr. Haaker opened the left hand wing emergency exit, "Mr. Garcia, the engineer, opened the right-hand wing emergency exit and each began launching a raft on the wings of the aircraft. I busied myself with checking to make sure that no passenger had been incapacitated or possibly partly hidden by debris. There was some debris on the floor such as parts of the ceiling which had pulled down. The tail had broken off and swung around to the left and was lying somewhat opposite the main cabin door."

Len Daniel tells what went on in the passenger compartment: "We were all in the braced position for an emergency landing; bent over at the waist with arms locked and tucked behind the knees. I remember the sound of crushing metal and our left wing dipping into the water. Then we came to a stop and there was absolute silence. The landing was over and I jumped up to begin opening the main cabin door and removing the life raft which was stowed to the left of the doorway. Then the door was opened and the life raft began inflating in the doorway as it wasn't totally out of the door, The engineer and I pushed and pulled frantically and nothing was happening.

"Finally after what seemed a long time Pat Reynolds came by and gave it a kick and out it went. Now I had to persuade people to step into the life raft. I was afraid to say too much fearing that the fear in my voice would give me away. I proceeded to go first and show the passengers how easily one could step into the raft and move to the other side. The rest of the passengers at the cabin door simply followed me.

"We were about eight or ten people in this life raft and noticed that we were unable to move away from the plane. The torn-off tail section had moved with the slight wave action and was pinning us in between the wing, fuselage and tail section.

" Someone suggested that we stand on the nearby wing and lift the life raft and put it in front of the wing. We did this easily. I saw passengers standing on the other wing taking pictures. I wanted to warn them that the airplane was sinking, but I realized that they probably knew this and decided pictures were more important."

For Dick Gordon, the memories remain sharp to this day.

"At last daylight came and we received our one-minute warnings. Everyone was quiet, although I remember telling Jane to hold tight and 'don't move your head.'

"The impact was loud and sharp. There was the noise of splintering as the tail of the plane snapped off and seats broke loose.

"Little Maureen, whom Jane was holding, flew out of her mother's arms into the bulkhead ahead of us. Her reaction, fortunately, was that of anger rather than pain.

" In a matter of minutes, three life rafts were pushed out of the remains of the plane and inflated, and we all made our exits according to plan. There was never any panic or loss of emotional control except on the part of the children, who were angry because their sleep was disturbed."

Mrs. Dix partly slipped into the water holding onto one of the Gordon twins and to a rope strung from the fuselage to an engine nacelle. She got to the raft safely. So did Herbert Ho who pushed off into the water and swam to the heavily loaded raft which held most of the women. They pulled him in and in a few moments the raft was half submerged. Its passengers, who included Katherine Araki and Mrs. Louise Walker, found themselves in water up to their shoulders.

From her raft. Pat Reynolds counted heads. Everybody was accounted for. She had lost one shoe in the ditching. She swung a wet silk—stockinged leg over the edge of her raft and kicked the other shoe high in the air. "We made it!" she yelled.

Gerry Henneman, a Pharmacist Mate on *Pontchartrain*, recalls: "It was like a dream. The plane circled once and began her final approach closer and closer, lower and lower. It looked like a smooth landing. After an eternity she touched, skipped, and then the terrific impact. The tail section wrenched off in an instant. Parts of the plane, probably the propeller, hurled over a hundred feet into the air and the terrible sound of it all. A sound almost impossible to describe. Some said that it sounded like a depth charge exploding.

"The concussion was felt even in the engine room. I can only say that it was the sound of impact, tearing metal, and explosion, all condensed into one. I've never heard a sound like that before and pray to God I shall never again. The plane nosed over in a great spray and settled in the ocean. A man standing near me cried out, 'My God, get those boats in the water.'"

BM3 Richard Olson's boat arrived at the plane before the passengers began to emerge. "We didn't know if anyone had survived the impact. Then we heard the wonderful sound of children crying! Not cries of pain, but the cries kids make when they're scared."

The first boat began picking up passengers within seven minutes after the plane touched down. Machinists Mate Second Class Ronald Christian jumped from the second boat up into the gaping bow section of the plane and made a thorough inspection of the interior, but found no one remained in the shattered cabin. The second boat then took aboard the occupants of the life rafts. *Sovereign of the Skies* sank five minutes after Christian left.

As the rescue boats were slowly picking their way through the crash debris, the *Pontchartrain* crew was ready to receive the survivors.

To those on the cutter it seemed an eternity before the boat tied up to unload its precious cargo. The first boat arrived with fourteen passengers—six men, six women and two children.

As the last boat was on its way back to *Pontchartrain* Bill Earle prayed: "Please God let there be seventeen aboard."

The crew began yelling out the count as the men and women climbed up the ladders,: fourteen, fifteen, sixteen," and finally, "seventeen!" A great cheer went up from the men on deck.

Within twenty minutes of the ditching, all 31 passengers and crew were aboard the cutter.

Earle left the bridge and came to meet Ogg.

"Captain Earle." said Ogg.

"Captain Ogg." said Earle.

They shook hands firmly.

Coast Guardsmen helped the passengers out of the rafts into the boats and brought them to the *Pontchartrain*'s Jacob's ladder. Crewmen were standing in a line, each one holding out a big white blanket in which to wrap them and asking, "Can I get you a cup of coffee?"

Those with apparent or reported injuries were taken to the Sickbay. The rest were taken to the Wardroom. There were five people with minor cuts or bruises. They were treated by Pharmacist Mate Henneman and Dr. Touzé.

Once everyone had been accounted for, Commander Earle went to the 1MC and choked out the words: "All saved! All saved!"

Seaman Apprentice Ronald Tepper stood by the Jacob's Ladder and helped Commander Strickler on deck. As the Commander stepped on board he proclaimed: "Thank God for the Navy." Tepper looked surprised, then smiled and tactfully replied: "Yes, sir. Thank God."

The little Gordon twins didn't have much to say about the incident. However, one of them, as she was being carried up over the ship's side and hurried below, was heard to remark to her mother, "Mommy, I don't like this hotel. It moves around too much. Let's not stay here."

Commander Earle concludes his narrative. " Captain Ogg said 'We are all mighty grateful to you and your men.' Though we had a great deal to say to each other, this was not the time. We talked briefly about the condition of the passengers and I invited him to join me for dinner that night,"

Feeling of Deep Pride

As *Pontchartrain* approached San Francisco Harbor three days later, another cutter met her and dropped off Coast Guard and Pan American officials, who brought along appropriate clothing for the survivors. Because they had lost everything in the airplane, they had been wearing Coast Guard-issued clothing.

Just inside the Golden Gate Bridge, *Pontchartrain* was met by fire boats spouting their water hoses, ships blowing their whistles and hundreds of small boats carrying welcome home signs. As they headed for the dock, a band struck up a lively tune and a great crowd surged forward amid popping flash-bulbs and panning television cameras.

Afterward

When the excitement had died down, Commander Earle received a letter from Captain Ogg. It read, in part: "I think you and your men are entitled to an unabashed feeling of deep pride as you contemplate your part in the episode. So I say again—thanks so much. Thanks, also, for the autographed picture of the Pontchartrain. This picture will remain a permanent and cherished part of my home." Captain Ogg's letter was framed and posted in the *Pontchartrain*'s Recreation Room.

The Civil Aeronautics Board Accident Investigation Report determined the probable cause of this accident was an initial mechanical failure which precluded feathering the No. 1 propeller and a subsequent mechanical failure which resulted in a complete loss of power from the No. 4 engine, the effects of which necessitated a ditching.

Also noted in the report is the following: "The Board believes that this report would be incomplete without a word of praise concerning the handling of this emergency by all the personnel involved. The Board highly commends the crew members for their ability in recognizing the malfunctions and taking correct emergency actions consistent with all known procedures. Their calm and efficient control of the situation averted what could have been a major air disaster.

In addition, the prompt response by the Coast Guard to the emergency and the immeasurable assistance rendered to the flight are deserving of particular praise."

Lessons Learned

Commander Earle summed it up best in his official SUPPLEMENT NO. 1 TO THE WEEKLY REPORT OF ACTIVITIES AND DEVELOPMENTS NO 145—56.

It is considered, on the whole, that this operation went off very smoothly. Since conditions were ideal, this is to be expected.

Nevertheless it demonstrated that considerable teamwork and integrated action is necessary, even under ideal conditions. It is believed that SAR Drills with airline personnel was an important factor contributing to this teamwork and another contributing factor was the live SAR Drill held by the PONTCHAR-TRAIN in conjunction with the CG Air Station in the San Diego area last August. This instruction and drill gave the new Commanding Officer and new Executive officer an immediate appreciation of the many factors involved, and provided valuable refresher training for the crew. One last contributing factor was the tremendous spirit of willingness and determination to succeed which was displayed by the entire crew of the ship. By separate correspondence I intend to call attention to particularly outstanding performances of individual officers and men so that they may be considered for appropriate official commendation.

There was no way of knowing at the time, but this was to be the last completely successful open ocean ditching in aviation history.

9. Epilogue

In preparation for landing, please return your seatback to the upright position and stow tray tables in the locked position.

While on final approach I'll tell you what happened to some of the people we've met during the flight.

USCGC *Bibb* and *Bermuda Sky Queen*

Chuck Martin continued flying, first for World Airways and then for Delta Airlines. Keith Woodmansee obtained a Flight Engineer license and later his commercial pilot's license, and finished his career flying for Pan Am.

Edgar Ritchie became Canada's highest ranking diplomat. He served as Canada's ambassador to Washington during the Johnson/Nixon years, returning to head Canada's department of foreign affairs (with the bureaucratic title of Undersecretary of State for External Affairs). He passed away several years ago. Gwen Ritchie is alive and living in Ottawa. She became an accomplished painter, both in oils and watercolors. In her wonderful account of the ditching Gwen wrote: "I do not believe that the average person is brave or is without courage by choice. I believe you can cope or you can't. If you can't, you appear to the world to be a coward. If you manage to summon up the strength to show courage, you will. Leadership produces courageous followers. On our own most of us succumb to our fears. In this accident it helped me a lot to be unafraid of the sea (a foolish trait I now believe) and it got me through the ordeal very well!"

As for Gordon Ritchie, he enjoyed a career in the Canadian public service, heading up the Department of Industry and he later negotiated the Canada-USA free trade agreement as Canada's ambassador for trade negotiations.

Mike Hall and James H. Macdonald had active careers in the Coast Guard and each retired with the rank of Captain. But for Mike it didn't end there. After retiring he obtained his Master Mariner's Certificate and captained merchant ships for several more years, retiring a second time in his mid-60s. However, there was yet another job to do when Saddam Hussein invaded Kuwait in 1990. Mike, then age 70, signed aboard as Second Mate on a freighter delivering supplies to US troops in the Persian Gulf before retiring for the third and last time.

USCGC *Bibb* served until 1985 when she was decommissioned. She and her sister ship, Duane, lay derelict for over a year at a dock in East Boston, Massachusetts before a unique opportunity arose for the two cutters to serve an honorable Final Duty as artificial reefs off Key Largo, Florida.

Mike Hall and Chuck Martin didn't meet while the Bibb was returning to Boston in 1947. It wasn't until August 2007 that they finally were brought together at Chuck's home in Georgia.

Thanks to Chuck Martin and Mike Hall, the Bermuda Sky Queen was and still is the greatest successful ditching in history.

Flying Tiger Airlines Constellation

Captain John Murray continued to fly for Flying Tiger Airlines after the ditching. He was given time off after the accident and the investigation. Ironically he died of a heart attack while swimming during a layover on Wake Island in 1966. He was by himself and there was no one to help him.

Sam Nicholson also remained with Flying Tiger Airlines until he was laid off when the airline replaced its navigators with inertial navigation systems. This happened in early 1971. He died of natural causes 25 or more years ago. He's remembered as a peach of a guy and funny to be around; he had a good sense of humor.

Carol Gould Hansen married her boyfriend shortly after returning to the states and currently lives in New Jersey.

Weather Patrols

Weather Patrols were long and monotonous for the thousands of Coast Guardsmen who manned the cutters. Now, more than 30 years after Ocean Stations were discontinued, their contribution to the safety of millions of airline passengers is largely forgotten. The crews remember and many of them gather every two years at the All Coast Guard Ships Reunion organized by Doak Walker (web site: http://www.255wpg.org). For a few days they swop stories and, once again, they become the youngsters who manned these obscure watery outposts.

USCGC *Pontchartrain* and *Sovereign of the Skies*

Commander Earle was later promoted to Captain and served many more years before retiring. He and Dick Ogg remained friends for years. Both Captain Earle and Captain Ogg died several years ago. Len Daniel Specia, Pat Reynolds Pimsner, and Frank Garcia are still with us and lead active lives.

The Gordons retired to Maryland many years later and the twins now have families of their own.

USCGC *Pontchartrain* was decommissioned on October 19, 1973 after 28 years of active service.

Real Heroes

Perhaps the real heroes of these stories are the aircraft. Whether on fire or torn apart by the implacable ocean, they stayed alive against all odds to save their human charges. Bermuda Sky Queen is in good company with Pan Am's Sovereign of the Skies, Flying Tigers' Constellation, Northwest's DC-7C, and Transocean Air Line's DC-4, among others.

Although each was blessed with a good crew, this alone can't account for why so many people survived. For me, there is no explanation other than the special relationship between man and machine that often occurs when lives are at stake.

End of the Flight

A completely successful ditching combines skill, training, and luck. Fortunately, ditchings rarely occur these days, but the need to prepare for one still exists for flight crews and passengers. As we've seen, it's often been the smooth coordination between everyone on board that's made the difference between life and death for many people. So, please listen to the flight attendant instructions so you'll know what to do in the event of a water landing.

We have now reached our destination. You may now unfasten your seatbelt and turn on any portable electronic devices. Thank you for flying with us and we look forward to seeing you again on future flights.

Copyright © Challenge Publications

Commercial Aircraft Ditching Summaries 1938 to 2009

1.   April 25, 1938
     Pan Am Sikorsky, S-43
     Kingston, Jamaica
     Damaged on take off
     4 crew and 12 passengers
     No casualties

2.   November 29, 1938—Ditched safely
     United Airlines DC-3
     Off Point Reyes, California
     Fuel exhaustion
     3 crew and 4 passengers
     2 survivors

3.   January 21, 1939—Broke up on impact
     Imperial Airways Short Brothers S-23
     North Atlantic
     Engines iced up
     4 crew and 9 passengers
     10 survivors

4.   October 31, 1945—Ditched Safely
     Air France, Laguna de Rocha, Uruguay
     The propeller of the Number 3 (left hand inboard) en-
     gine separated killing 2 passengers
     Unknown number of passengers and crew
     2 fatalities

5.   January 11, 1947—Ditched Safely
     Far East Airlines
     Pacific Ocean
     An in-flight fire in the no. 2 engine.

5 crew and 37 passengers
7 fatalities

6.   January 22, 1947—Ditched safely
      TACA de Columbia DC-3
      Santay Island, Ecuador
      Engine fire
      Unknown number of crew and passengers
      No fatalities

7.   October 14, 1947—Ditched safely
      American International Airways *Bermuda Sky Queen*
      North Atlantic
      Fuel exhaustion
      7 crew and 62 passengers
      No fatalities

8.   August 15, 1949—Ditched Safely
      Transocean Air Lines DC-4
      Shannon, Ireland
      Fuel exhaustion
      9 crew and 49 passengers
      8 fatalities which included one crew member

9.   June 5, 1950—Ditched Safely
      Aviation Corporation of Seattle Curtis C-46
      Atlantic Ocean
      Engine failure
      3 crew and 62 passengers
      28 fatalities

10.   April 11, 1952—Ditched Safely
      Pan Am DC-4
      San Juan, Puerto Rico
      Engine problems
      5 crew members and 64 passengers
      52 fatalities

11. June 19, 1954—Ditched Safely
     Swissair Convair CV-240
     English Channel
     Fuel exhaustion
     4 crew and 5 passengers
     3 fatalities

12. March 26, 1955—Ditched Safely
     Pan American Airways Boeing 377 Stratocruiser
     Engine failure
     35 miles off the Oregon coast
     23 persons on Board
     4 fatalities

13. April 2, 1956—Ditched Safely
     Northwest Airlines Boeing 377 Stratocruiser
     Puget Sound, 4.7 nautical miles southwest of Seattle-
     Tacoma Airport
     Engine failure
     6 crew and 32 passengers
     5 fatalities

14. October 16, 1956—Ditched Safely
     Pan American Airways Boeing 377 Stratocruiser
     Sovereign of the Skies
     Pacific Ocean
     Engine failure
     7 crew and 24 passengers
     No fatalities

15. July 14, 1960—Ditched Safely
     Northwest Airlines DC-7C
     Philippine Islands
     Fire in the left wing and loss of the No. 2 propeller
     7 crew and 51 passengers
     1 fatality

16. July 14, 1960—Ditched Safely
     Philippine Air Lines DC-3
     Between the islands of Negros and Mindanao
     Fuel exhaustion
     3 crew and 28 passengers
     No injuries

17. September 23, 1962—Broke up on impact
     Flying Tiger Line Lockheed Constellation
     North Atlantic
     Engine fire
     8 crew and 68 passengers
     28 fatalities

18. October 22, 1962—Ditched safely
     Northwest Airlines DC-7C
     Sitka Sound, Alaska
     Engine failure
     7 crew and 95 passengers
     No injuries

19. August 23, 1963—Ditched safely
     Aeroflot Tupolev Tu-124
     Neva River, Leningrad
     Fuel exhaustion
     52 persons on board
     No injuries

20. May 2, 1970—Ditched Safely
     ALM DC-9
     Atlantic Ocean Princess Juliana International Airport,
     Saint Maarten
     Fuel exhaustion
     63 occupants
     23 fatalities

21.   August 7, 1980—Ditched Safely
      Tarom Romanian Airlines Tupolev 154B-1
      Mauritania.
      Landed short of the runway
      152 passengers and 16 crew
      1 fatality due to heart attack

22.   November 23, 1996—Broke up on impact
      Ethiopian Airlines 767
      Comoros Islands
      Hijacked
      12 crew and 163 passengers
      123 fatalities

23.   January 16, 2002—Ditched Safely
      Garuda Indonesia Boeing 737
      Bengawan Solo River near Yogyakarta, Java Island
      Landed short of the runway
      6 crew and 54 passengers
      1 fatality—a flight attendant drowned in less than 3
      feet of water

24.   August 6, 2005—Ditched Safely
      Quinter [Tuninter] ATR 72
      Off the Sicilian coast
      Fuel exhaustion
      4 crew and 35 passengers
      16 fatalities

25.   January 15, 2009   Ditched Safely
      US Airways Airbus A320
      Hudson River in New York City
      Bird strike
      155 passengers and crew
      No fatalities

About the Author

After graduating from Montclair State College with a B.A., Mike served in the U.S. Coast Guard for six years as a commissioned officer and a senior petty officer. His assignments included buoy tending, search and rescue missions, search and rescue coordination, drug law enforcement, and oceanographic operations in the Arctic. As part of the Boarding Party and Prize Crew on two cutters he participated in the seizures of a Panamanian drug-runner and a Cuban fishing boat.

Mike's first book, *Bloodstained Sea: The U.S. Coast Guard in the Battle of the Atlantic 1941-1944*, was published by International Marine, a division of McGraw-Hill, and received critical acclaim by reviewers and veterans. The Naval Order of the United States honored him with its 2005 Samuel Eliot Morison Award for Naval Literature. *Bloodstained Sea* is now available through Cutter Publishing.

On the lighter side, he published, in conjunction with Flat Hammock Press, a new edition of *Sinbad of the Coast Guard*, the adventurous, true story of the USCGC Campbell's mascot whose exploits during World War II became legend. Appropriately, Sinbad's story was told by a fellow member of the Coast Guard, Chief George F. Foley, Jr., while the fine pictures were drawn by the outstanding Coast Guard Reserve artist, George Gray.

Mike's first novel *Choke Points* (Cutter Publishing, 2009) addresses the real threats to Maritime and Port Security. It's the first of a ten-book Fletcher Sage series spanning 250 years.

He is a contributing author to the US Naval Institute's Naval History Magazine as well as regularly posting articles on Authors Den.

In 2005, Mike appeared on the History Channel series Man, Moment, Machine episode about Andrew J. Higgins, the designer and builder of the vital landing craft used in World War II, and, as a script consultant for the episode, reviewed the material for accuracy. In 2010 he will be one of the subject matter experts on a PBS documentary about the U-boat war off the US east coast during WWII.

In different venue, Mike has produced a new version of the old song "I'd Like to Find the Guy Who Named the Coast Guard," originally written and recorded by Paul Yacich and the Coast Guard Band in 1945. The music has been lost, but working with Alison Freemen, Mike has given a new lease on life to this wonderfully humorous tune and updated it with three verses reflecting today's Coast Guard global missions.

His expertise includes such diverse fields as leadership, international terror, trans-national crime, human trafficking, piracy and counter piracy operations as well as geo-political and military history.

He can be reached through his web site: www.mikewalling. com.

Endnotes

1. Introduction

1) Department Of Commerce Report Of Aircraft Accident Investigation, July 2, 1938.

2) Air Safety Board, Civil Aeronautics Authority, February 18, 1939.

2. Bermuda Sky Queen

3) Unless otherwise noted the information for this chapter includes:

    a. US Coast Guard interviews with Captain Paul Cronk and Tina Lewin;

    b. US Coast Guard Alumni Bulletin, and public domain sources including USCGC *Bibb* logbook, October 1947 and Report of Assistance dated October 14-19, 1947; and

    c. Captain Paul B. Cronk, "The Rescue On Station Charlie," *The Atlantic Monthly*, July1950: 37. Reprinted with permission

4) Sources: Keith Woodmansee's Diary and excerpts from "The Dunking Of The Queen," *The Radio Officers' News*, May 20, 1949, Volume XVIII. Reprinted with permission

5) Gwen Ritchie, "Bermuda Sky Queen according to Gwen Ritchie." Reprinted with permission.

6) KHFOG de NMMC QRK K Translation : "Aircraft Calling this is Bibb, What is the intelligibility of my signals? Over"

7) NC. 18612 QAB VOAC INSUFFICIENT FUEL-RETURNING TO NMMC FOR EMERGENCY LANDING AT SEA. 62 PASSENGERS 7 CREW, . . QSW 4220 A3 8280 CW"

"Bermuda Sky Queen, I have clearance for Gander but have insufficient fuel—returning to Bibb for Emergency Landing at sea.... Will you send on this frequency 4220 or on 8280 Continuous Wave (Morse Code)?

8) "Rescue On The North Atlantic" by Phil Taylor. Reprinted with permission.

9) "A Tsarist Officer in the US Coast Guard" by Mike Walling. George Vladimirovich Stepanoff was the son of Vladimir and Katherine Stepanoff and born in Moscow, Russia on April 23, 1893. Little is know about his early years except that his parents were Vladimir and Katherine Stepanoff and, in 1919, he was an Imperial Russian Navy officer stationed on board a Second-class Russian cruiser (destroyer) in Vladivostok.

During the Bolshevik Revolution Stepanoff remained loyal to Czar Nicholas and become part of the White Russian forces in the Pacific. In 1919, American, British, Canadian, and Chinese troops occupied Vladivostok. Ships from these countries as well as France controlled the port. The story, as told by Mike Hall, is Stepanoff and his fellow shipmates seized two Second-class cruisers in 1918 and sold them to the Japanese. The tale gains credibility by the fact that five Tverdi-Class destroyers were seized by White Russian forces and two, Tochni (*Tochnyi*) and *Tverdi* (*Tviordyi*), were transferred to the Japanese sometime between 1919 and 1920.

Apparently Stepanoff used some of his share of the sale to buy passage to the US. He then enlisted in the US Coast Guard on December 5, 1923 as a Boatswain's Mate First Class. His first assignment was on board the newly commissioned tug *Shawnee* (WAT-54) stationed in San Francisco, California. By 1941 he had been promoted to Chief Boatswains Mate and was commanding officer of *Raritan* (WYT-93) based in Staten Island. Shortly after taking command, Raritan became part of the Greenland Patrol Forces based in Narsarssuak. While there he was promoted to lieutenant. Following three years in Greenland Stepanoff returned to the States, taking command of USS *Might* (PG-94), one of the ten Canadian corvettes transferred to the US Navy as part of the reverse Lend-Lease. Following VE Day, Stepanoff, now a Lieutenant Commander, was assigned to *Algonquin* (WPG-75) out of Portland, Maine.

Following *Algonquin*, Stepanoff when on to command *Argo* (WPC-10), *Laurel* (WAGL-291), *Spar* (WLB-403), and *Yamacraw* (WARC-333) interspersed with short assignments to Base Boston until retiring May 1, 1955. In all, he served for twenty-two and a half years, not counting possibly as much as ten years in the Tsar's Navy. During his service he was awarded the American Defense Service Medal with letter "A", American Campaign Medal, Asian-Pacific Campaign Medal, WWII Victory Medal, European-African Middle Eastern Medal, and National Defense Service Medal.

After retiring, he lived with his wife Valentina in Ayer, Massachusetts. George Vladimirovich Stepanoff, Commander, USCG (Retired), died March 8, 1980, was cremated, and his ashes buried in Mt. Auburn Cemetery, Cambridge, Massachusetts.

<u>Author's Note</u>: I first heard about CDR Stepanoff from Mike Hall, Captain, USCG (Retired), who served with him on *Algonquin* and afterwards Mike and Stepanoff became good friends. By the time they met, Mike had been in the Coast Guard for four years, almost all of which was spent at sea and most of that time on board *Spencer* during the Battle of the Atlantic (see *Bloodstained Sea* for more about Mike Hall). Mike feels he learned more from CDR Stepanoff than virtually anyone else and still has a deep respect for his one time CO.

From what I know of Mike, he and CDR Stepanoff are cut from the same cloth. Both preferred sea-going assignments to being on shore, are leaders in the best sense of the word, are exceptional seaman, and have little tolerance for incompetence or bureaucracy. Sadly, there are few if any like them left today.

10) Civil Aeronautics Board Accident Investigation Report (File No. I-0088), December 14, 1948

3. Flying the Oceans

11) Centennial of Flight

12) Smith, Richard K., *First Across*, Naval Institute Press, Annapolis, MD, 1973

13) However, the first commercially successful trans-Atlantic flights where made by German Zeppelins (dirigibles) beginning in October 1928. For almost nine years zeppelins were the only means of crossing the Atlantic by air. In the following year, *Graf Zeppelin* undertook a number of trips around Europe, and following a successful tour to Recife, Brazil in May 1930, it was decided to open the first regular transatlantic airship line. This line operated between Frankfurt and Recife in 68 hours, and later, between Frankfurt and Rio de Janeiro, with a stop in Recife. Despite the beginning of the Great Depression and growing competition from fixed-wing aircraft, *Graf Zeppelin* transported an increasing volume of passengers and mail across the ocean every year until 1936. On March 4, 1936, *Hindenburg*, the largest airship ever built, made her first flight. However, in the tense political situation of German re-armament, helium to inflate it was not available due to a military embargo. So, in what ultimately proved a fatal decision, the *Hindenburg* was filled with flammable hydrogen. On May 6, 1937, the *Hindenburg* burst into flames while landing in Lakehurst, New Jersey. The fire and following crash killed 35 of the 97 people on board and one member of the ground crew.

14) The luxurious service ended in June 1940, when the routes to the Empire were finally severed by the global expanse of World War II.

15) Excerpts from Century of Flight *Flying Boats*. Reprinted with permission.

16)   On January 11, 1938, Musick took off from Pago Pago pilot-
      ing the Samoan Clipper to begin a survey flight and soon af-
      ter the flight began, he reported an oil leak in engine number
      4. In an attempt to assure a safe landing, he made the fateful
      decision to dump fuel in order to lighten the plane . The deci-
      sion proved disastrous when fuel vapors collected in the wing
      structure causing the plane to explode in mid-air. The US Navy
      ship Avocet recovered the scattered remains of the clipper that
      evening.

17)   In 1937 Fred Noonan resigned from Pan Am. A short time later
      he signed on as the navigator for Amelia Earhart's attempted
      round the world flight. They were last seen in Lae, New Guinea,
      on July 2, 1937, before disappearing over the Central Pacific
      Ocean on their next eastward leg to Howland Island.

18)   Bells are rung every half hour in four hour cycles (12-4, 4-8,
      and 8-12,). One bell is struck for each half hour. For example
      10:30 is five bells struck in the following sequence: ding-ding,
      ding-ding, ding.

19)   *ETOPS Explained*, Section 5 "ETOPS Across the Atlantic," by
      Boeing Commercial Airplanes. This is a Boeing Commercial
      Airplanes informational white paper that has been fully cleared
      for external release in 2007. Reprinted with permission

20)   *ETOPS Explained*, Section 6 "ETOPS Across the Pacific," by
      Boeing Commercial Airplanes. This is a Boeing Commercial
      Airplanes informational white paper that has been fully cleared
      for external release in 2007. Reprinted with permission.

21)   Air Safety Network, Flight Safety Foundation

22)   ibid

23)   Sources:

      a. Norman Sklarewitz, "Terror on a Pacific Night," , *Saturday
         Evening Post*, January 21,1961, Vol. 234, No. 3. Reprint-
         ed with permission of Curtis Publishing

      b. Civil Aeronautics Board Aircraft Accident Report, File No.
         1-0026, Released November 23, 1962

24)   *FLIGHT,* 22 July 1960, reprinted with permission.

25)   ob cit

4. Navigation

26)   "Atlantic Ditching," Arby Arbuthnot, *TARPA Topics*, June
      1984. Reprinted with permission.

27)   Civil Aeronautics Board Accident Investigation Report, File
      No: 1-0086, Released
      September 15, 1950.

5. Ocean Weather Stations

28)   Parts excerpted from *The Story of the Coast Guard Weather Sta-
      tions* by Bernard C. Natly and Truman R. Strobridge, US Coast
      Guard Academy Alumni Bulletin, March/April 1974, Vol.
      XXXXI. No. 2. Reprinted with permission.

29)   On September 4, 1941, at 8:40 A.M. the U.S. Navy Destroyer
      Greer (DD-145), carrying mail and passengers to Argentia, was
      signaled by a British plane that a U-boat (later identified as
      U-*652*) had crash-dived some 10 miles ahead. Forty minutes
      later *Greer's* soundman picked up the under seas marauder, and
      Greer began to trail. The plane, running low on fuel, dropped
      four depth charges at 10:32 A.M. and returned to base, while
      Greer continued to dog the U-boat. Two hours later U-*652* be-
      gan a series of radical maneuvers and *Greer's* lookouts could see
      her pass about 100 yards off. At 12:48 P.M., the U-boat turned
      and fired a torpedo at her pursuer. Ringing up flank speed, the
      destroyer turned hard left as her crew watched the torpedo pass
      100 yards astern. Then charging in *Greer* laid a pattern of eight
      depth charges, and less than two minutes later a second tor-
      pedo passed 300 yards to port. *Greer* lost sound contact dur-
      ing the maneuvers, and began to quarter the area in search of
      the U-boat. When the encounter ended two hours later, *Greer*
      had dropped nineteen depth charges and U-*652* had fired two

torpedoes. Although no damage was done to either ship, the shots blew away the last vestiges of U.S. neutrality in the North Atlantic.

When news of this attack against an American warship on the high seas reached the United States, President Franklin Roosevelt seized on the occasion to make one of his Fireside Chats. Declaring that the German attack had been an act of piracy, President Roosevelt further stated: "in the waters which we deem necessary for our defense, American naval vessels and American planes will no longer wait until Axis submarines lurking under the water, or Axis raiders on the surface of the sea, strike their deadly blow first." From then on U.S. warships were to shoot on sight any German warships they encountered. The United States' undeclared war in the Atlantic moved to a new, deadlier phase.

30)   14 USC—U.S. Code—Title 14, 3—Sec. 3: Coast Guard (January 2004): Upon the declaration of war or when the President directs, the Coast Guard shall operate as a service in the Navy, and shall so continue until the President, by Executive order, transfers the Coast Guard back to the Department of Homeland Security [NOTE: In 1941, the US Coast Guard was under the Department of the Treasury].

31)   U-755 was sunk in the Mediterranean by a Royal Air Force Hudson on May 28, 1943. Nine of the U-boat's crew of forty-seven survived the attack and were rescued by the Spanish.

32)   The number and location of ocean weather stations, originally determined by the Weather Bureau in consultation with the commercial airlines, were during the war determined by the cognizant committees under the Joint Chiefs of Staff, primarily the Meteological Committee of which the Weather Bureau, but not the Coast Guard was a member. With the establishment of the Air Coordinating Committee, that body recommended and approved the number and location of the stations.

33) Reprinted with permission from *Alpha, Bravo, Charlie...Ocean Weather Ships 1940-1980* by Robertson P. Dinsmore, Woods Hole Oceanographic Institution Marine Operations, Oceanus Magazine, Posted December 1, 1996

34) John Van Dyke, Merchant Navy Nostalgia, Ocean Weather Ships, http://iancoombe.tripod.com/id56.html. Reprinted with permission.

35) Commercial Aviation March 30, 1939

36) "Transport: Muddling," *Time Magazine*, Monday, February 6, 1939

37) Narrative Report Of The Rescue Of Survivors Of U. S. Air Force Plane , 27 April 1949 By USCGC SEBAGO (WPG-42). Commanding Officer, USCGC SEBAGO (WPG-42), 28 April, 1949

38) Reprinted by permission of Captain Henry C. Keene, Jr., USCG (Retired)

6. Ditching

39) Patrol Squadron 6 (VP-6), Naval Aviation Museum (http://www.naval-air.org/flightlog/squadrons/vp-6.htm)

40) "A History of Coast Guard Aviation, The Growth Years 1939-1956", John "Bear" Moseley (http://www.uscg.mil/history/webaircraft/CGAviationHistoryIntro.asp)

41) This information has been extracted from an older version of Appendix H of the *National Search and Rescue Manual*. The information and diagrams have been deleted from the current manual.

42) This relationship between sea condition and wind speed is found in the Beaufort Scale, created in 1806 by Sir Francis Beaufort and used by mariners ever since.

43) ob cit

44) Department of Transportation, Federal Aviation Administration, Advisory Circular, Passenger Safety Information, Briefing And Briefing Cards, Dated July 23, 2003, AC No. 121-24C

45) Reprinted with permission from Wendy Stafford, Flight Attendant Express, www.cabincrewjobs.com, "What to expect from flight attendant training, part 2"

46) Landing Ty-124 to Neva (ПОСАДКА НА НЕВУ), reprinted with permission from A.P.Ivanenko, The chief of Historic-archival Department DOS, Aeroflot Headquarters, Moscow, Russia

47) Pilot saves lives by landing on a river…in 1963," Source: http://www.russiatoday.com/features/news/36011

48) The Stars and Stripes, European Editions, Volume 21, Number 10, September 25,1962 and Volume 21, Number 164, September 29, 1962. Reprinted with permission.

49) Sources:

    a. *The Ditching of NWA 293: The unknown story of a breathtaking rescue off the coast of Alaska in 1962* by CAPT David V. V. Wood, USCG (Ret.), IN SERVICE BEYOND,April 2009. Reprinted with permission

    b. Northwest Airlines *INCIDENT OF DITCHING OF NWA DC-7 AT SITKA, ALASKA*.Reprinted with permission

c. Civil Aeronautics Board Aircraft Accident Report, File No. 1-00030, NORTHWESTAIRLINES, INC., DC-7C, N 285, DITCHING *** SITKA SOUND, ALASKA, OCTOBER 22, 1962. Released: September 19, 1963.

50) Alaska Standard Time is one hour earlier than Pacific Standard Time thus, 12:25 P.M. Alaska Time is 1:52 P.M. Pacific Time.

51) A Check Pilot accompanies AIR PLANE CAPTAINS (air trans.) and AIRPLANE FIRST-OFFICERS (air trans.) periodically, to test and review their proficiency: Observes and evaluates pilot knowledge and skills, utilizing such means as technical manuals, check lists, and proficiency tests. Notes compliance with and infringement of company or Federal Aviation Administration flight regulations. Compiles and issues reports on findings

to appropriate company and Federal Aviation Administration officials. Source: Webster's Online Dictionary.

7. Faith, Birds, and Hijacking

52) Sources: Aviation Safety Net, http://aviation-safety.net/database/record.php?id=20050806-0

53) National Transportation Safety Board. 2010. *Loss of Thrust in Both Engines After Encountering a Flock of Birds and Subsequent Ditching on the Hudson River, US Airways Flight 1549, Airbus A320-214, N106US, Weehawken, New Jersey, January 15, 2009.* Aircraft Accident Report NTSB/AAR-10 /03. Washington, DC.

54) The U.S. Centennial of Flight web site lists the date as May 1930.

55) New World Encyclopedia, http://www.newworldencyclopedia.org/entry/Hijacking

56) Sources: U.S. Centennial of Flight Commission Aviation Security (http://www.centennialofflight.gov/essay/Government_Role/security/POL18.htm) and Wikipedia

57) Sources include:

   a. Criminal Acts Against Civil Aviation 1996, US Department of Transportation, Federal Aviation Administration;

   b. "Ethiopia's own Superhero Pilots Leul Abate and Yonas Mekuria, Ethiopian Airlines Public Relations Office Release, January 18, 2009.

58) `I Thought I Had Finished My Life'—Tale Depicts Drunken Abductors Who Fought With Pilot—Survivors Tell Of Terror As Jetliner Tumbles Across Ocean's Surface*
AP: Washington Post, Monday, November 25, 1996. Reprinted with permission.

59) *Honeymooners capture dramatic images of Ethiopian jet crash*, CNN , November 26, 1996.

8. Sovereign of the Skies

60)   Sources:

    a.   Civil Aeronautics Board Accident Investigation Report, File No. 1-0121, Released July 11, 1957

    b.   *Thank God For the Navy*, LT. (jg) JAMES A. FROST, First Lieutenant, USCGC *Pontchartrain*

    c.   U. S. Coast Guard Magazine December 1956

    d.   *The Ditching of Pan American Flight 943*, by Mary E. "Lynn" [sic] Daniel Specia, April 30, 2005

    e.   Statement of Richard N. Ogg, Captain, N90943/B377 Ditching, October 16, 1956

    f.   DITCHING, a pilot's view, by Captain Richard N. Ogg, Pan American Airways, April 1957

    g.   "One Minute to Ditch!, The untold human story behind the headlines," Cornelius Ryan, *Collier's*, December 21, 1956. p. 26. **Author's Note**: A search of the US Copyright Office records on-line records did not show this article to still be under copyright either by Collier's or Cornelius Ryan. A similar internet search also failed to show any current copyright ownership. If this is incorrect please let me know immediately as to who does own the copyright so that I may contact them.

    h.   Letter from Gerry Henneman, Pharmacist Mate, USCGC *Pontchartrain* Sent to Pat (Reynolds) Pimsner, October 1956

    i.   Supplement No. 1 To the Weekly Report Of Activities And Developments No 145—56, Commander William K. Earle, USCG

    j.   "All saved!" The story of a rescue at sea, *PAA Clipper*, Volume 3, Number 1, Summer 1997

    k.   Dick Gordon's narrative of the ditching. Reprinted with permission